SPORT CLIMBING

TECHNICAL SKILLS FOR
CLIMBING BOLTED ROUTES

The author on 'Alice', 7a,
St George, Switzerland

ABOUT THE AUTHOR

Pete Hill MIC, FRGS has climbed in many continents and countries across the world, including first ascents in the Himalayas. He is a holder of the MIC award, the top UK instructional qualification, and has been delivering rock and mountain sports courses at the highest level for a number of years. He is a member of the Alpine Club, honorary life member of the Association of Mountaineering Instructors and a Fellow of the Royal Geographical Society. A lack of common sense has caused him to be found on the north faces of the Eiger and Matterhorn in winter, as well as on a number of other extreme routes climbed in difficult conditions in the European Alps, Africa, Nepal and India. He spends a lot of time travelling to European sport-climbing venues in search of sunshine and the ultimate route.

Pete lives in Scotland and has two daughters, Rebecca and Samantha. A frequent contributor to various magazines and websites, he is also author of *The International Handbook of Technical Mountaineering* and *Rock Climbing: Introduction to essential technical skills*, and co-author (with Stuart Johnston) of the globally successful *The Mountain Skills Training Handbook*. He runs both summer and winter skills courses from beginner through to advanced level, and can be contacted via his website at www.petehillmic.com.

SPORT CLIMBING

TECHNICAL SKILLS FOR CLIMBING BOLTED ROUTES

by

Pete Hill MIC, FRGS

CICERONE

2 POLICE SQUARE, MILNTHORPE, CUMBRIA, LA7 7PY
www.cicerone.co.uk

ACKNOWLEDGEMENTS

As always, I'm indebted to friends, acquaintances and others who have eased the passage of this project through their unselfish help and support. Samantha Hill took the climbing photo on page 4, and Giles Stone is responsible for the one on page 65. For the 'Selected Sport-climbing Venues' section, Jonathan Preston, Allen Fyffe and Rob Johnson kindly let me use some of their climbing photographs of Italy, the USA and Spain respectively, and Scott Muir endured my leaning over his shoulder to take photographs during a bolting expedition to 'crag x'; my thanks to all of them. The topos in the guidebook section are taken with permission from the excellent *L'escalade dans les Alpes-Maritimes*, and I am grateful to Jean-Claude Raibaud and those involved in Alticoop for letting me do so. Giles and Fran Stone provided a base in the south of France for my climbing trips in the sun, loosely disguised as 'research'; thanks are due to them for their hospitality and seemingly inexhaustible supplies of red wine. Equipment support was generously supplied by a number of companies, with particular thanks to Frank Bennett at Lyon Equipment (www.lyon.co.uk), Beal for the ropes and software (www.bealplanet.com), Petzl for the hardware used in photographs (www.petzl.com) and Faders for the excellent SUM (www.faders.es).

Finally, Paula Griffin once again burnt the midnight oil trying to make sense of my often illegible scratchings and for that – as well as being the perfect climbing partner – I am eternally grateful.

Front cover: Les Fees Meres, 6b, Saint-Jeannet, Maritime Alps

CONTENTS

NOTE

To avoid confusion when describing sequences of moves involving a climber and second, the use of 'they' has been avoided. Instead 'he' is used to refer to the leader, and 'she' to refer to the belayer/second.

INTRODUCTION

Sport climbing has become phenomenally popular over recent years. From its early days when those drilling rock were castigated by traditional climbers, most now accept that sport climbing has its place alongside crags where leader-placed protection is the norm. The increase in personal leisure time and the explosion in low-cost air travel have done much to encourage the growth of the sport. Travel to some of the hottest cragging spots in the world is now possible at a fraction of the cost, in real terms, of 10 years ago.

'Sport' climbing differs from 'traditional' climbing in that, generally, the protection used to safeguard the leader is already in place, in the form of bolts and rings drilled into the cliff. Unfettered by a large rack of wires, chocks and camming devices, the climber carries little more than a few extenders, and is free to climb fast and hard, pausing only briefly to clip the gear as he passes by. Climbers often find that they can climb far harder than their usual traditional leading grade, as the security of a well-bolted and user-friendly crag induces a relaxed atmosphere and thus an improvement in performance.

This style of climbing is often seen as having a 'minimalist' approach, where extra kit often only comprises shorts, T-shirt and sunglasses. Although bolted routes are found the world over, it is this 'sunny' aspect of many sport-climbing venues that is a great attraction to many. To be able to combine a climbing trip or holiday with some well-bolted sport routes somewhere with stable and predictable weather makes for an excellent change to what may otherwise be a mundane, workaday routine.

This book sets out the variety of skills needed to complete a bolted route safely. At many levels the skills base is low, and simply being able to belay and clip in an extender correctly, allied with the knowledge of how to organise a lower-off, will give a great day out. However, as grades and length of routes increase – in particular when dealing with multi-pitch climbs – it is essential to have more technical knowledge. This book will take you all the way from the basics, such as tying on and belaying, through the skills needed to climb safely on multi-pitch crags the world over.

Whatever your aspirations, make sure you have a good – and safe – time on the crag. Sport climbing is here to stay. Hopefully those who still see it as a 'dark art' will change their opinion before long and realise that climbing, in all its forms, is big enough for everyone to have their own space, enabling us all to get on with what is important – having fun.

(Opposite)
Climbing 'Paracouerte', 4+, Bernard Gobbi, France

1

BOLTS AND BOLTING

Well-placed close bolts

1 BOLTS AND BOLTING

A 'bolt' is a generic, cover-all term used to describe a piece of metal protection fixed to a rock face. There are many different styles and types, and which one to use in any particular location will depend upon a number of factors. Rock type, location (coastal or inland), local ethics, type of climbing and the financial situation of the bolter all play a part.

TYPES

The majority of bolts can be categorised into three main styles of placement:

- **Glue-in bolts** – provide a very strong protection point that will last for years if placed correctly.
- **Hammer-in** or **screw-in bolts** – ready for immediate use, whereas a glue-in style bolt has to be left to cure for a period of time before being loaded.

The placement of bolts is fairly easy to achieve, although it does take experience to position them appropriately and in context with the moves of the route they are going to protect. Placing them badly is even easier: missing out crucial bolts on crux sections, placing them under bulges with little thought as to the run of the rope, or right on the lip of roofs where repeated falls could weaken the very rock into which they are drilled.

Glue-in bolts come in a variety of shapes and sizes. The commonest will consist of a lightly threaded shaft and a D-shaped head. In terms of width 10mm and 14mm are the most usual, with those around 70mm long being used in hard rock types, and 100mm long in softer rock. Some glue-ins look like a large staple, and need two holes drilled in the rock in order to seat them properly.

A **hammer-in bolt** will often be used by those who are protecting technical climbs at altitude or on very long, technical routes, because neither spanners nor similar tools are needed to place them. The bolt comes as a single unit. A post protrudes from the hanger down the centre of the bolt. Once the hole has been drilled and the bolt placed in it, the post is driven in with a hammer. This expands the outer casing of the bolt, causing it to grip the drilled hole internally.

Two glue-in resin bolts used as an anchor. The threaded shaft allows for a better grip with the adhesive.

A very common style of expansion bolt seen on sport routes is the **screw-in bolt**, where a nut assembly is turned, drawing a stud through the centre of the bolt, causing it to expand and jam in the drilled hole. These are very quick to place and can be used immediately, a bonus if a climber wishes to equip a route and climb it the same day.

LOWER-OFFS

Generally, the tops of routes are equipped with points from where climbers can lower off or abseil. Although there are variations, these can be placed in two broad categories:

- Where you can clip in the rope and go down.
- Where you need to untie the rope from your harness and thread it through before descending.

Lower-offs can consist of either one or two bolts, sometimes joined together with a chain or similar linkage, sometimes not.

Expansion bolt: exploded view below, full bolt above

(Top left) **Common two-bolt and chain rig lower-off, equipped with a thread-through ring**

(Top right) **Clip lower-off with a chain from two glue-in bolts**

(Bottom left) **Common configuration for a two-bolt lower-off**

(Bottom right) **Tail-shaped single-point lower-off**

Tip

It is extremely important that you satisfy yourself that the bolts on the route you are about to climb are well placed and appropriate for the job in hand. If you have any doubts as to the security of the placements, go and climb somewhere else. Factors that may determine whether you climb or not, having examined the protection, may include the following:

- Evidence of rusting, such as rust streaks under the placement, particularly on sea cliffs.
- Bolts that have been damaged.
- Bolts not placed flush with the rock.
- Any glue-ins that do not display signs of glue at the outer edge of the drilled hole.
- Bolts that move.
- Rotating hangers.
- Bolts placed in areas of loose rock.
- Bolts placed very close to the lip of a roof.
- Bolts or hangers that are obviously home-made.

(Above) **Old bolt and hanger: treat with suspicion as you do not know how deeply the rust has penetrated**

(Below) **Very poorly placed bolt with damaged head and hanger**

Rusty chain and bolt – be wary!

Rusty old peg, certainly not to be trusted

Home-made bolt, fashioned out of a bent metal bar

EQUIPPING A ROUTE

Although I am not going to go into particularly technical detail about the specific mechanics used when placing a bolt, it is interesting to have some background knowledge about how this is done. Assuming that the route has been chosen, the next decision is whether to bolt upwards or downwards. This will depend upon a number of factors, such as the provision of anchors at the top of the proposed route and how steep it is. It will often be best to descend the route, drilling as appropriate on the way down. On a very steep route this is useful as the rigger can use the rope clipped through an extender on the previously drilled bolt to hold him close to the rock as he prepares the next one down. The following photographic sequence shows the stages of equipping a steep sport route with expansion bolts.

← STEP 1
Any loose rock near the placement is prised off and the area cleaned. Note the drill hanging on the abseil rope, out of the way but easy to access.

EQUIPPING A ROUTE

↓ STEP 4
The placement is finished off by using a spanner or torque wrench. Care must be taken here – too loose or too tight will both weaken the placement.

↑ STEP 3
The bolt and hanger is placed into the hole and hammered snugly into position.

↑ STEP 2
The hole is drilled at an angle of 90° to the rock.

(Left)
Poorly placed glue-in bolt: the head should be flush with the rock. Treat all such placements with extreme caution.

(Opposite)
Clipping a glue-in bolt on limestone, Turbie, south of France

The placing of glue-in bolts is treated a little differently, as these cannot be used for a period of time while the glue, or resin, sets. This can take as little as 20 minutes through to four days, depending on the type of fixative used and the ambient air temperature.

1   A hole is drilled into the rock at precisely the correct location, width and depth.
2   Any loose material such as dust is cleaned out by blowing and using a bottle-brush.
3   Many glue-in bolts are supplied with a handy capsule of glue, ready to go. This is placed in the hole.
4   The bolt is then placed into the hole and driven in whilst being rotated so that the glue completely covers the light thread on the shaft.
5   Any excess glue is wiped away from the outside of the hole, and the placement is left to cure for the recommended time period.

EQUIPMENT

Apart from the bolts, a rigger's gear will consist of a few decidedly non-technical-looking bits of kit. Out-of-the ordinary gear will include spanners, a torque wrench, rags, hammer or old ice axe, and a drill. The drill will normally be a heavy-duty battery-powered industrial hammer type, capable of making short work of a variety of rock types. In some circumstances, however, the rigger may have no option but to use a hand-held drill operated by striking the back of it with a hammer. This has the effect of rotating an internal mechanism at each blow, which in turn rotates the drill bit. The obvious disadvantage is the time and effort that it takes to drill a hole. This style of hand drilling is very useful where the location is remote and there is no chance of carrying in a heavy industrial drill, or where it could be used as a back-up should the drill battery fail and none other be available.

Battery drill and associated paraphernalia for placing bolts

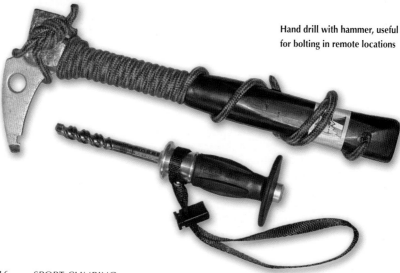

Hand drill with hammer, useful for bolting in remote locations

EQUIPMENT

Tooled up and ready to go

2 EQUIPMENT

One of the attractions of sport climbing for many climbers is the minimal amount of equipment needed to complete a climb effectively and safely. Rope, harness and extenders are the basics, which – along with rock boots and belay device – will enable many routes to be completed. However, there is also plenty of other gear available – you have to decide what 'extras' you really need to take with you. The following information may help you decide.

Harnesses

Personal preference will determine what sort of harness you choose. One recommendation is that the harness has a sewn central abseil loop at the front. This allows for easy belaying and abseiling with minimal fuss, and ensures that the harness is loaded correctly by linking the leg loops and waist belt in the right manner. Sport-climbing harnesses will usually be lightweight with fixed leg loops and few 'extras', although a good racking system is important. If routes are to be worked over a period of time and a number of falls possible, pick a harness with sufficient padding. However, remember that excessive padding will be hot and sweaty, so aim for a compromise between comfort when climbing and comfort afforded by good air circulation. Try on several different styles in the shop, and if possible hang in them for a couple of minutes – quite a few establishments are set up for this.

A good sit harness, with padded leg loops and adjustable belt

Belay seat

For very long routes, which may entail periods of time when the belayer hangs from intermediate stances, a belay seat could useful. This takes the weight off the thighs and back, enabling more comfortable belaying. The commonest types consist of a ripstop nylon or similar fabric construction, cut and sewn into a triangular shape with tapes at the corners. When the belayer sits in the seat, two tapes go either side of the body, with another running up through the legs, and are then clipped into the anchor. The belay seat is there to assist with comfort; the harness – the main load-bearing and safety part of the system – is at no point undone. Although a useful piece of kit, it's only worth carrying one if you are certain that you are going to spend some time hanging from stances.

Belay seat, which rolls up into its own useful carrying pouch

Helmet

Although often overlooked as a necessary piece of equipment on sport climbs, a helmet will protect the head in the event of a fall as well as from debris dropping from above. Although some climbers will choose to do without one, the wearing of a helmet is highly recommended at all times, especially when tackling multi-pitch routes and those with intricate abseil descents. Some routes finish below a band of loose rock, and in this situation wearing a helmet is sensible. Many of the designs available today are so lightweight you'll barely notice you're wearing one.

Modern helmets are lightweight and very strong

Rope

Choice of rope will often depend on the length, style and difficulty of the routes to be climbed. However, a general-purpose rope needs to be long enough to allow routes to be completed and the climber safely lowered off, light enough not be a hindrance, and have properties that allow it to absorb energy in the event of a fall. Single-rated 60m ropes of 9.5–10.5mm diameter would be a good choice for both single and double-rope climbing. The thinner the rope the less practical life it will have if handled roughly. If you are going for a lot of single-pitch routes involving both leading and bottom-roping, a thicker rope would do; for multi-pitch or higher grade routes a thinner and lighter one would fit the bill.

Rope bag

This is a useful piece of kit that helps to keep expensive ropes clean, dry and protected from harmful grit. Most designs consist of a rucksack-style bag, which opens out to give a large piece of tough material, perhaps measuring 1.5 x 2m, onto which the rope is placed. Each corner will have a sewn loop, two of which are usually coloured red and green. One end of the rope is secured to one of the loops, and the rope run through and placed in a large pile on the mat. The other end is secured to another loop and the whole lot rolled up and stored in the attached rucksack, and so carried from route to route. When arriving at the crag, the mat is unrolled from the rucksack, flattened out, the top end of the rope is untied and the leader ties directly on.

Ensure that the rope is completely dry when rolled away at the end of the day; if there is any doubt it should be dried before being placed in the rucksack. Good quality rope bags will also allow the carrying of rock boots, extenders and one or two other climbing essentials along with the rope.

Belay devices

The many belay devices available are suitable for both sport routes and for traditional climbing. Belay devices can be arranged into two general categories:

- **Passive** Very common; usually consisting of two slots through which ropes can pass, although the use of just one rope is more usual with sport routes. Many designs will have an extended groove on the 'dead' side of the device, often mildly ribbed. This is designed to add friction in the event of a fall by helping to grip the rope, and is very handy when using a rope with a narrow diameter.

- **Active** Often the choice of climbers attempting hard routes where a number of falls or rests will be made. Although not a 'hands-off' design, they allow the belayer to be more relaxed when the device is loaded, with the mechanism itself holding most of the climber's weight. Common examples are the Grigi and the SUM.

Belay devices:
gripping (left),
passive self-locking (centre)
and active self-locking (right)

If an abseil descent is to be made, a passive belay device will normally be chosen over an active one. As the abseil rope will be doubled to allow for retrieval, passive devices allow both sides of the rope to be controlled via the two slots. Active devices normally only allow for the control of one rope, making the arranging of abseils a little more awkward and time-consuming.

Chalk bag

Although not strictly essential, many climbers will feel naked without one of these. Also, the harder sport climbs may not be possible without the extra friction that chalk provides, in particular when allied with crags prone to becoming hot during the day. Personal preference will determine which product you buy. A fleece lining helps disperse the chalk, and a tightening cord prevents it from spilling out in transit. The opening should be large enough to allow your hand easy entry. Remember that this will be a little more difficult if you wear the bag behind you – try it out in the shop first. A tape tunnel to enable a carrying belt to be attached, or a karabiner loop for attachment to a harness, is essential. Many models incorporate a slot for carrying a small nylon brush for cleaning holds.

Chalk

The commonest way of buying chalk (magnesium carbonate) is in a block, which can be broken down into a powder as required. Some is sold ready powdered, often in cardboard tubes that can be used to top up a chalk bag. Chalk balls – powdered chalk contained in a small mesh bag – are very popular, and normally the only type allowed on climbing walls as spillage is kept to a minimum. Chalk comes in many colours, and climbers in some areas use chalk tinted to match the rock on which it is being used. The use of chalk should be carefully considered, because – due to its abrasive quality – overuse can result in the polishing of holds. In particular, its use on easy routes that receive a lot of traffic should be discouraged as all natural friction in the rock is removed over a period of time.

Extenders

The ultimate choice of extenders – also called quick-draws – is down to the individual. However, most will choose shorter extenders than those used on traditional routes, as a bolt line will often be relatively straight. Extenders which are 10cm long are commonly used, with 15cm the next most popular choice. Longer routes, or those where leader-placed protection may be encountered, might entail the carrying of extenders measuring 20cm or more to help reduce rope drag.

Extenders: the shorter version will often be the choice for clipping bolts on sport routes, with a couple of longer ones useful for off-line bolts

The thickness of the tape has little bearing on the final strength of the gear, and will only make a slight difference to the overall weight if many are carried. Some designs use a wide tape for durability, thinner at the point where the karabiner clips in. The rope end of the extender is often furnished with a rubber retaining loop designed to hold a karabiner rigid, which can assist when making quick or awkward clips.

Snapgate karabiners

The snapgate karabiners used on the extenders will need to be as light as possible, with wire gates generally contributing to weight saving. Most often, climbers will choose to have a straight gate at the bolt end and a bent gate at the rope end. The bend to the gate allows for easier and more positive clipping of the rope when making awkward clips. Bent gates should never be clipped into a bolt as they could undo in certain circumstances, such as if rotated by the movement of the rope.

If extenders and their karabiners are to be used for both bolted routes and traditional climbing, it makes sense to have a set of karabiners for use just on bolts. The inside curve at the end of the back bar can become nicked or burred, perhaps during a fall onto a sharp bolt hanger. If this karabiner was subsequently used in a situation where rope or tape was run through it, the burr could damage the soft fibres of the rope. If identical karabiners are used at each end of the extender, mark one of them with tape to ensure that it is always clipped into the bolt to help avoid the burring problem.

Karabiner damaged by a bolt hanger. Care must be taken that it is not used on the rope end of an extender.

HMS and D-shape screwgate karabiners

Sometimes referred to as a pear-shape karabiner, an HMS is identified by the wide curve at one end. This avoids the sharp angle created at the end of the back bar (part of the design of normal D-shape karabiners), allowing for the use of the Italian hitch (see Chapter 3) in a far more efficient manner than would be possible with 'D' shapes. Using the hitch on the D-shape design could result in it jamming during a lower, for example, leaving both climber and descender stranded.

Having said this, D-shape karabiners are very strong and can be used for other jobs, such as arranging anchors, as bottom-rope connectors and for secure running belays. A rack of gear will therefore often have two HMS and four or so D-shape karabiners on it.

EQUIPMENT

HMS karabiners: some makes have a red band by the sleeve, a useful indicator to check if they are locked properly

Frog

This device is a variation on a standard extender. It has a short sewn sling with a bentgate karabiner on one end, but the other end has a grasping mechanism designed to be pushed vertically upwards onto a bolt hanger. When it touches the hanger, two arms clip shut, securing it with a scissor-like action. One of the attractions of a frog is that the climber can be a little distance below the bolt and still

Frog, which allows a bolt to be clipped from underneath

efficiently clip it, gaining a few centimetres over a conventional extender. Although quite heavy, a frog is a useful addition to a standard rack of extenders, although it will be found that the opening isn't quite wide enough to clip onto the largest gauge of ring-bolt.

Wires

Longer routes may require the carrying of a few wires. It may also be worth carrying some on the back of the harness on single-pitch climbs if the crag is known to have marginal or questionable bolt placements. Only carry a few – maybe five or six – and make sure they are as lightweight as possible. Should areas of blank rock be encountered, this protection may make the difference between success and failure. They are also useful for backing up bolts with damaged hangers.

Camming devices, chocks, slings

Some routes will be poorly equipped with bolts, or may just have lower-off stations provided with no bolts along the line of the route. In this case all intermediate runners will have to be placed by hand during the ascent. It is rare for this to happen without it being made clear in the relevant guidebook that the route requires leader-placed protection, and this style of climbing tends to be found on routes taking meandering lines up remote faces. A standard selection of equipment should be available, although many guidebooks will specify if certain sizes of cam, for example, are required, or if wires provide the only protection. The decision whether to carry a rack of equipment can be made before leaving home by studying the appropriate guidebooks, possibly allied with local knowledge or an Internet search.

Slings

Slings come in many widths, sizes, materials and colours. The commonest uses are:

- As a cow's-tail
- To rig a bottom rope (see Chapter 5)
- To equalise anchors on a multi-pitch route.

A thick construction is good for the first two examples as it will endure wear and tear well. The anchor sling can be of a thin material such as Dyneema or Spectra, which does not have the abrasion resistance of its thicker cousins but is still very strong, lightweight and easy to work with when tying knots. A cow's-tail sling is usually around 60cm long (measured doubled when laid flat), a bottom-rope rigging sling can be 120cm long, and an anchor sling 240cm. Although there are many variations in usage, and subsequently in design and length, these are the most useful to start out with.

Cow's-tail

This very important piece of kit is used to secure the climber to an anchor, most commonly when threading the climbing rope through a top chain or similar, prior to being lowered off. It can be made in a number of ways:

- By using a 60cm sling lark's-footed around the abseil loop of the climber's harness and furnished with a screwgate karabiner, which is left clipped in to a gear loop during the ascent.
- By using a sling called a 'daisy chain', which has a number of loops sewn in it, so that the distance from the anchor can be varied.
- By using a short section of offcut climbing rope, with one end tied around the front of the harness as you might do with the main climbing rope. The other end will have a loop tied in it, most often done with a figure of eight knot, and a screwgate.

Clip stick

Clip sticks are now frequently seen, although sometimes frowned upon if used on certain crags, and known in some circles as a 'cheating stick'. However, a clip stick is sometimes the only way to get a rope and extender onto a crucial low bolt and protect the climber from a potentially dangerous fall at the start of a route. It may also be used in the event of a redpoint ascent, where the climber uses the stick to progressively clip bolts until the lower-off is gained, ready to practise the route prior to making a full ascent.

Cow's-tail attached to the abseil loop on a harness and clipped into a gear loop ready for use

Clip sticks are often home-made from a length of wood or metal, onto the end of which an extender can be connected with the rope already attached. A telescopic paint roller handle be converted into an excellent clip stick. In its simplest form the karabiner can be held in place with a

small piece of tape, strong enough to hold the extender and rope but weak enough to pull apart once the bolt has been clipped and the stick pulled down. Other home-made versions include a mousetrap-type device, where the karabiner is held in place with a spring, or can be made by utilising the plastic gate-keeper from a karabiner such as the DMM belay master. This plastic clip can be fixed to the top of the pole, and is a good size for accepting many dimensions of karabiner.

Commercially made clip sticks tend to be lighter than home-made versions, and will extend to around 5m. They have a cunning device at the end to hold the karabiner in place, keeping the gate open until the last moment. Some will have a carrying loop, which can be clipped onto the climber's harness for when the stick is being used for redpointing (see Appendix 3: Glossary) or clipping a number of bolts along the line of a route.

Clipping a bolt using a clip stick

Spare karabiner for lowers

On longer routes, and for those with questionable bolt placements, you may have to be lowered off before completing the pitch. In this situation having a spare karabiner clipped to the back of the harness is useful, as it will stop you from having to sacrifice an expensive extender or karabiner. The spare can be almost any type, and will often be the one found in a dusty corner at the bottom of your gear cupboard. An excellent alternative is a small maillon, which can live unobtrusively at the back of the harness until needed, and will be cheaper to sacrifice. A maillon also has the advantage that its opening can be screwed shut, avoiding any unexpected unclipping of the rope during preparation for descent.

Maillon closed *(left)* **and open** *(right)*

Prusik loop

In order to protect an abseil, the carrying of a prusik loop is recommended. This will normally only be necessary on multi-pitch routes or single-pitch crags where abseil descent is required. The loop is best fashioned from 6mm accessory cord, and should be in the region of 40cm in diameter when tied with a double fisherman's knot (see Chapter 3).

3 KNOTS

Few knots need to be learned for sport climbing. In many situations you can get away with simply knowing how to attach yourself to your harness securely. However, as with all aspects of climbing and mountaineering, it is very helpful to know a little more than just the essentials. This will ensure that, should problems or unexpected situations arise, you will be equipped to deal with them in an efficient manner.

Rewoven figure of eight

This is very useful for attaching you to your harness, and has a distinctive shape once completed. When tying on with a rewoven figure of eight, the loop created by the rope should ideally end up no bigger than the abseil loop on the harness. If there is no abseil loop, make the rope loop a little less than fist size. Once tied, it is worth finishing the eight off with a stopper knot, either an overhand or half a double fisherman's knot. The left-over tail should only be around 5cm long, with the stopper butted up snugly against the figure of eight.

REWOVEN FIGURE OF EIGHT

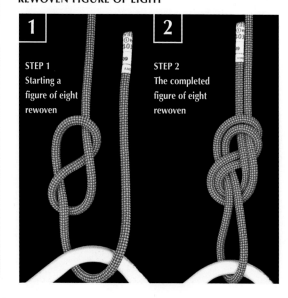

1

STEP 1
Starting a
figure of eight
rewoven

2

STEP 2
The completed
figure of eight
rewoven

Figure of eight on a bight

This version of the figure of eight is reserved mainly for use when tying onto a belay stance, when the anchor is out of reach. It is quick to tie and has the advantage of not needing any karabiners for connection to the belayer. It also has some dynamic properties, meaning that it tightens up when loaded, reducing the impact force on the belay system.

Another version is just tied onto either the end or a loop of the rope. This is very useful when lowering off as a karabiner is clipped in, connecting the rope to the climber's harness. It should be finished off with a stopper knot, such as half a double fisherman's.

Double bowline

This is a good knot for tying onto your harness, and similar in design to the single bowline. Although the rewoven figure of eight has, in many quarters, overtaken the bowline, the double version is a very useful knot to learn. Its main advantage is the ease with which it can be untied once it has been loaded. For this reason it's often used by climbers who are leading at the top of their abilities, where a number of falls may be taken before the route is completed.

Once the double bowline has been tied, it is absolutely essential that a stopper knot (half a double fisherman's) is then used to secure the tail end of the rope. This will prevent the main knot loosening and inverting itself; if this happens it could fail. The stopper knot should be tied so that it is butted up snugly against the bowline as it is tightened. Finally, check that the entire knot has been tied correctly.

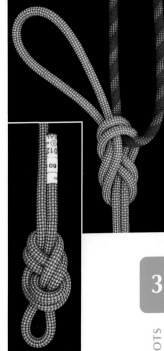

(Above right) **Figure of eight on a bight**

(Above left) **A figure of eight on a bight, suitable for attaching the rope to the climber's harness**

DOUBLE BOWLINE

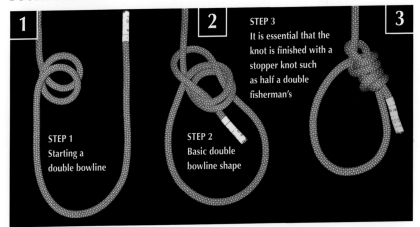

1

2

3

STEP 3
It is essential that the knot is finished with a stopper knot such as half a double fisherman's

STEP 1
Starting a double bowline

STEP 2
Basic double bowline shape

ITALIAN HITCH

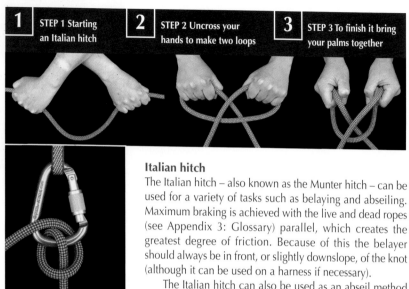

1 STEP 1 Starting an Italian hitch

2 STEP 2 Uncross your hands to make two loops

3 STEP 3 To finish it bring your palms together

4 STEP 4 Completed Italian hitch

Italian hitch

The Italian hitch – also known as the Munter hitch – can be used for a variety of tasks such as belaying and abseiling. Maximum braking is achieved with the live and dead ropes (see Appendix 3: Glossary) parallel, which creates the greatest degree of friction. Because of this the belayer should always be in front, or slightly downslope, of the knot (although it can be used on a harness if necessary).

The Italian hitch can also be used as an abseil method (see Chapter 10), although if the end of the rope is not hanging free it will tend to cause the ropes to twist when used for a long descent.

The Italian hitch can be tied with one hand if necessary, perhaps when the belay karabiner is situated at arms' length above a stance. If the karabiner has its gate opening to the right, clip the rope into it so that the rope from the belayer is running up from the back of the krab and through the front to your harness. Using your right hand (as below) grasp the rope at the back, reaching past the front rope on its left-hand side. Bring that rope forwards and, without twisting it, place it through the gate of the karabiner.

ONE-HANDED ITALIAN HITCH

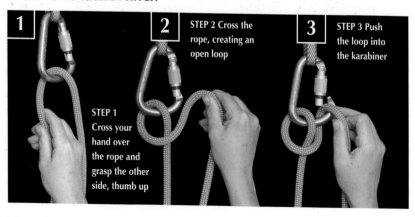

1 STEP 1 Cross your hand over the rope and grasp the other side, thumb up

2 STEP 2 Cross the rope, creating an open loop

3 STEP 3 Push the loop into the karabiner

Tip

The Italian hitch should always be used in conjunction with a pear-shape or HMS screwgate karabiner. This style of krab has been designed to allow the hitch to rotate freely around its wide end, enabling the unhindered taking in or paying out of the rope. If the hitch is placed into a D-shape karabiner, with a sharp angle at the lower section of its back bar, there is a chance that the hitch will jam when the rope's direction of travel is altered.

Clove hitch

The clove hitch has a particular place as a belay knot, both for ground anchors and for stances on multi-pitch climbs. It is simple to tie, simple to adjust and locks itself tight when loaded.

The hitch is best clipped into an HMS karabiner, which allows it to sit in the correct manner.

With some practice the clove hitch can be tied into a karabiner with one hand. This can prove very useful when clipping into an anchor system on steep ground, where a hold on the rock or anchor chain is needed with the other hand. This will require a little thought beforehand, otherwise you may end up with a lark's-foot, Italian hitch or simply a couple of wraps of rope around the karabiner.

If the karabiner has its gate opening to the right, clip the rope into it so that the rope from the belayer is running up from the back of the krab and through the front to your harness. Using your right hand (as below) grasp the rope at the

CLOVE HITCH

STEP 1
A clove hitch is started the same way as an Italian hitch, but place one hand behind the other without twisting

1

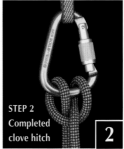

STEP 2
Completed clove hitch

2

ONE-HANDED CLOVE HITCH

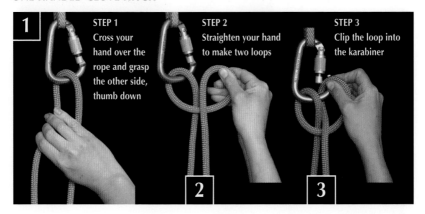

1

STEP 1
Cross your hand over the rope and grasp the other side, thumb down

STEP 2
Straighten your hand to make two loops

STEP 3
Clip the loop into the karabiner

2

3

back, reaching past the front rope on its left-hand side. Rotate your hand anticlockwise as you do so, so that your palm is facing to the right. Bring the rope forwards, straightening your hand. Now bring the loop you have created in front of the remaining rope and round into the gate of the karabiner.

French prusik

Particularly good as an abseil back-up knot, the French prusik has the advantage over a number of other knots tied in a similar fashion in that it can be released whilst under load. This is crucial, not only when abseiling but also when constructing emergency systems. Fashioned with a prusik loop, the joining knot tied to form the loop should be kept away from the wraps around the main rope, otherwise the holding power of the hitch could be compromised. The prusik loop is neatly wrapped around the rope a number of times, depending on the intended use, whether it is around one rope or two (as in abseiling), whether the rope is new and slick or old and furry, and so on. Both ends of the prusik loop are now clipped into a karabiner. A load applied to the karabiner causes the wrappings to tighten and distort a little, making them grip the rope.

To release the French prusik under load, for example in an abseiling situation, place your hand above the knot and pull down on the loops along the line of the main rope, using the tips of your fingers.

French prusik. Keep the wraps neat around the main rope.

Tip

As with any knot tied using a prusik loop, any shock loading of the system must be avoided. If not, there is a chance that catastrophic failure may occur as the knot may slip a short way and either burn through or strip the sheath of the climbing rope.

Double fisherman's knot

This knot is useful in the construction of equipment, such as fashioning prusik loops. It can also be used to tie two climbing ropes together when abseiling. Tying just part of the knot – half a double fisherman's – will give you an efficient stopper knot, essential when tying onto a harness with either a figure of eight or a bowline.

DOUBLE FISHERMAN'S KNOT

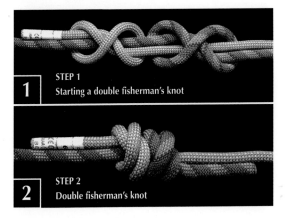

1 STEP 1
Starting a double fisherman's knot

2 STEP 2
Double fisherman's knot

Overhand knot

The overhand knot can also be used as a stopper knot, although half a double fisherman's is preferable. Another common use is when using slings to equalise anchors, such as at a stance or when linking two bolts at a lower-off for a bottom-roping session.

Overhand knot

Lark's-foot

The lark's-foot is not a particularly strong knot and has few uses, but is very appropriate when attaching a sling to a harness in order to fashion a cow's-tail for clipping onto a lower-off chain or similar.

To link the sling to the harness, thread it though the leg loops and waist belt to create a small loop, then thread the other section of the sling through this. A karabiner can be clipped into the sling in readiness for clipping into an anchor. As an alternative, the lark's-foot can be tied around the abseil loop.

Lark's-foot on a harness, used here to make a sling into a cow's-tail

Turbie, near Monaco

4 BASIC SKILLS

This chapter will cover the basic skills needed for a climb to take place as well as looking at some of the more technical procedures, such as equalising anchors, which will be useful as you progress.

WHAT HAPPENS WHEN YOU CLIMB A ROUTE?

To those used to traditional climbing – where a leader goes up a route and then brings the second up, after which the pair either walk off or abseil back to the base – sport climbing will appear a little different. Let's take a typical, single-pitch bolted sport route and see how it works.

1   The leader climbs the route, clipping runners into the pre-placed bolts.
2   The top of the route may be well below the top of the crag, as it is unusual to 'top-out' in the traditional sense. There will be a lower-off point provided, and the leader arranges the rope through it.
3   The leader is lowered down by the belayer, stripping out the extenders as he descends.
4   The team swaps over; the belayer becomes the climber and bottom-ropes the climb.
5   Once he has reached the chain, he is lowered off to the ground.
6   The team pulls the rope through and moves onto the next route.

This may be a simplistic way of looking at a climb, but this is an extremely common process, repeated at sport-climbing venues all over the world. There are, of course, variations to this sequence, such as:

• Once the original leader has lowered off, the rope is pulled through and the second climber can lead the route, clipping the bolts in the normal way.
• The original leader is lowered off and leaves the extenders in place. The rope is pulled through and the next climber ascends, clipping the pre-placed gear.

Those used to traditional multi-pitch routes will be used to the process in a multi-pitch situation. This will usually be one of the following:

• The leader climbs the first pitch, is joined by the second, then continues up the second pitch and so on.
• The leader climbs the first pitch and brings up the second, who then becomes the leader for the next pitch. This is called 'leading through' or 'swinging leads'.

However, a couple of things in sport climbing may be new to traditional climbers:

• The provision of *in situ* gear at the stances, allowing for quick clipping in and belaying.
• Often, the line of descent will be down the route just climbed, using the equipped stances as the abseil stations.

TYING ONTO THE ROPE

There are several ways in which the rope can be attached to the harness. The least satisfactory is by use of a screwgate karabiner, which connects a figure of eight knot in the end of the rope to the abseil loop on the harness. This may work for short sections of bottom-roping, but you must be sure that the karabiner will remain in the correct position on the harness and that there is no possibility of it unscrewing by being dragged against the rock, or twisting so that it would be loaded sideways in the event of a slip.

Clipped onto the rope using two screwgate karabiners back to back. DO NOT use this method for leading.

Look at the manufacturer's recommendations (supplied when you bought the harness) about how to connect yourself should you wish to use the screwgate method. Most will recommend the use of two screwgates, facing opposite directions, to help counter the chance of accidental unscrewing or inappropriate loading.

Tip

The use of a screwgate karabiner – or even two – to connect the climber to the rope in a leading situation should never be contemplated, as the chance of a sideways loading in the event of a fall would seriously weaken the strength of the connection.

Tied on with a figure of eight rewoven and half a
double fisherman's stopper knot

Tied on with a double bowline and half a double
fisherman's stopper knot

The normal method of attachment, whether bottom-roping or leading, will be by tying in, either with a rewoven figure of eight or a double bowline (see Chapter 3). Which one you use comes down to personal preference, although there are a couple of slight differences. The figure of eight is instantly recognisable, so when checking each other prior to starting the climb you may find it easier to see if something has gone awry. The double bowline, on the other hand, has the advantage of being easy to untie once it has been loaded. This is a useful consideration if you are pushing your grade and trying hard routes, taking a number of falls as a consequence.

Note

It is essential that with either a figure of eight or a bowline a stopper knot is tied to secure the knot in place. By doing this, you are ensuring that the main knot cannot work loose, which can be a problem, particularly with the bowline.

Make sure that the correct section of the harness is threaded prior to tying the knot. The line the rope takes will usually be that followed by the abseil loop, through the leg loops and around the waist section. Once tied (figure of eight or bowline) try to get the resultant rope loop about the same size as the abseil loop. Any larger than roughly fist size and there is a chance it may catch on gear during the climb.

CLIMBING CALLS
It is very important to be clear about what is happening at all stages of a climb. There are set sequences of climbing calls that are universally understood, in particular when dealing with traditional routes, where topping out is the norm. When a single-pitch sport route requires the climber to be lowered back to the ground, a number of these calls become redundant and others must take their place. For clarity, the usual sequence of calls is as follows:

'Taking in'	From the leader at the top of the route, as he pulls up all the slack between him and his second
'That's me'	From the second, when the rope is tight
'Climb when you are ready'	From the leader, once he has placed the second on the belay and has checked the system
'Climbing'	The second is ready to start, but does not climb until confirmation comes from the leader
'OK'	The leader confirms that he has heard the second, and starts to belay

This is an extremely sensible progression of calls, clarifying what is happening between the two climbers, and is still relevant for multi-pitch sport routes. However, for single-pitch routes, where the climber is going to be lowered to the ground, a different version can be used. Although the final decision will be up to the team, they will most likely use something along the following lines:

'Safe'	From the leader, once he has reached the lower-off and has clipped in his cow's-tail
'Take in'	From the leader, once he has arranged the rope at the lower-off. This will be at the point where he pulls himself tight onto the anchor in order to check the tie-in, just prior to unclipping the cow's-tail
'Down'	The leader is ready to descend

Various other calls and commands are in general use. Some of the more common are:

'Runner on'	From the leader when he clips the first bolt, so that the belayer knows it's time to start paying attention
'Take in'	Said on the route, meaning that the climber needs some of the slack rope to be taken in through the belay device
'Slack'	The rope is too tight and the climber needs a little more in order to complete a move
'Tight'	The climber needs a hand from the rope, and a tug will often help him over a difficult section, both physically and psychologically

(continues on p40)

4

BASIC SKILLS

'Watch me'	The climber is about to make a difficult move, or is about to fall off, and this is a method of reassuring himself that the belayer is being attentive
'Take'	Said a split second before the climber falls off or commits his weight to the rope
'Rope'	Called before either deploying a rope down a crag for abseiling or climbing, or when retrieving a rope at the bottom of the crag, after the climber has been lowered off and the rope is about to be pulled through the anchor
'Below'	A loud shout if a rock or other debris has been knocked down from the top of the crag or an intermediate ledge – a good reason to wear a helmet

EQUALISING ANCHORS

There are a number of reasons why being able to efficiently equalise anchors would be a very useful skill to acquire.

- It may be that a lower-off consists of two unlinked bolts, and you wish to spend time bottom-roping the route. Simply running the rope through the two bolts would solve the problem, but to have each point taking 50 percent of the load would be a better arrangement.
- Alternatively, the stance on a multi-pitch route may only be furnished with two separate bolts, and you need to link them together to provide security for your second coming up, as well as a safe belay point for the pitch above. Again, tying directly in with the rope would help to solve this, but should you be leading the entire route and not swapping leads with your second, this method would be a bit cumbersome.

Equalising anchors has two advantages:
- It presents you with a single attachment point, into which you can clip yourself and run a direct belay from.
- It ensures that any load is shared equally between the bolts, very useful where bolts are of questionable age and strength.

A sling will usually be used to equalise anchors. As bolts are never too far apart, a sling with a 120cm measured length (often called an '8-foot' sling) will normally do the job. However, it may be wise to carry a 240cm ('16-foot' sling) instead, as it will reach further should the anchor points be some distance apart. Some climbers carry a length of thin

Tip
....

Although an overhand knot is the quickest to tie, think about what the sling is going to be used for. If it is part of a bottom-rope system – and in particular if the sling is made from a thin Dyneema or Spectra material – the overhand knot will be extremely difficult to undo once it has been loaded. Instead use a figure of eight on the bight, or even a figure of nine (one more half-turn). These knots will be easier to undo once the system has been finished with and stripped down. This is relevant to both the above method as well as the clove hitch system detailed below.

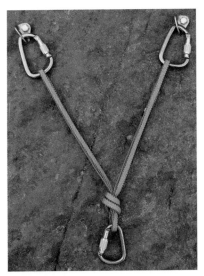

Two anchors equalised using a sling tied with an overhand knot

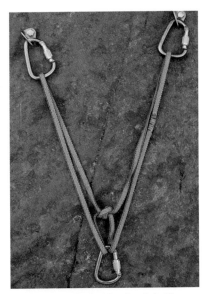

Two anchors equalised with a sling tied with an overhand knot that separates it into two sections

rope tied into a loop for this purpose, but you may find that the convenience and lack of bulk of a ready-sewn Spectra or Dyneema sling will be preferable.

For the following methods of equalising anchors, we will assume that the lower-off is equipped with two good bolts, set a short distance apart from each other. They need to be furnished with screwgate karabiners, or at least two snapgates in each, arranged to open in opposite directions.

Overhand knot on a bight method

This is the commonest way to equalise anchors, is easy to remember and looks 'right' once it has been tied.

- The sling is clipped into both the screwgates, and they are done up.
- Grasping both sections of the sling from between the bolts, pull it down in the direction that the load will be taken, for instance the line that the bottom rope will take.
- At this point, tie an overhand knot on the bight in the sling.
- This loop is now the point into which you will clip any karabiners needed for the system to run.

Single overhand knot method

This uses less sling length than the method described above and can be useful if the bolts are set a little further apart. It does look as though it won't work, however! Just take a second to check that it has been clipped correctly and all will be fine.

- One end of the sling is clipped into an anchor.
- An overhand knot is tied loosely around the sling at the position you think the load point will be.

- The other end of the sling is clipped into the second screwgate.
- The overhand knot can now be adjusted to the point of loading and then tightened.
- This has created two small loops, one to each anchor. Clip a screwgate through each of these independent loops and use it as required.

Clove-hitch method

This is included here for completeness. It does not use too much sling, but you may feel that it is much more fiddly than the two methods above, and so will choose to ignore it. However, it is highly adjustable, useful if you need to alter your position slightly, for example when your second reaches the stance on a multi-pitch route. Don't use this method for rigging a bottom-rope system as the clove hitches tighten excessively around the karabiners – particularly when using thin slings – and untying them can be awkward.

Two anchors equalised using a sling with two clove hitches and an overhand isolation knot

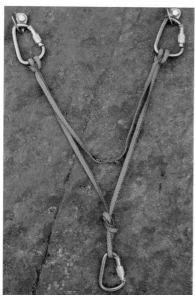

- A clove hitch is tied in the sling and clipped into one of the screwgates on the anchor.
- A second clove hitch is clipped into the other bolt, with a small amount of slack between the two. This allows for later adjustment if needed.
- The long loop of sling that now hangs down has an overhand knot tied in it, and this becomes the attachment point. Ensure that the knot is tied so that each anchor is loaded equally.

Two-sling method (1)

If the bolts creating the anchor are some distance apart, or you are only left with a couple of short slings, it is still possible to equalise the system.

- Clip a sling into each of the anchor points.
- Tie an overhand knot at the point where the longer sling reaches the lower point of the shorter one.
- Clip your karabiner into the shorter sling and into the longer one above the knot.
- The knot can be adjusted up or down a little as required.

Equalising two anchors using the two-sling method (1)

Two-sling method (2)

If the attachment point needs to be above the point reached by the shorter sling, the following method is appropriate.

- Clip a sling into each of the anchor points.
- Hold the slings together at an appropriate point and tie an overhand knot in both.
- The screwgate karabiner now clips into the slings above the knot. Ensure that it is through the correct part of the slings and not just clipped between them.

An alternative to the second method is to tie an overhand knot in each sling at an appropriate point to shorten them, and clip a karabiner into both.

Self-adjusting sling method

Using this method it is possible to clip a sling into two anchor points and have it self-adjust, with the attachment karabiner sliding along the sling to wherever the loading point is centred. This can work well, but should only be used where there is no question whatsoever about the solidity of the anchor bolts. If one should fail, the set-up of the system means that the attachment karabiner would slide to the end of the sling and shock-load the second bolt. If this is of questionable strength, it too may fail under the increased loading. As the attachment karabiner is mobile (as when using this set-up for bottom-roping) heat can be generated at the crossover point of the sling to which the karabiner is attached. For this reason, it is recommended that a thick sling be used, as a thin lightweight sling could be damaged by any heat generated by the movement.

For these reasons, it may therefore be preferable to use one of the other systems detailed above. However, as this method is sometimes seen in use, it is included here for completeness. Personally it is my least favourite and I steer clear of it.

Equalising anchors using the two-sling method (2)

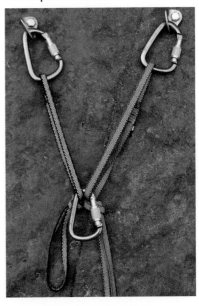

Two slings tied together with an overhand knot in each to equalise two anchors

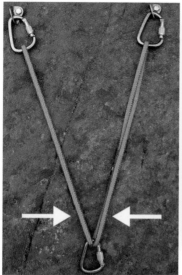

Three anchors equalised with a sling and overhand knot

Two anchors joined with a self-equalising sling system

- The sling is clipped into both bolts.
- Holding the two sides of the sling at the lowest point, cross one over the other and clip in a screwgate karabiner.
- Make sure that the karabiner is held captive by the sling and not simply clipped around it. The system can now be used.
- Two overhand knots, one each side of the attachment point and a few centimetres away, will help to reduce the shock load on the remaining anchor should the other fail. These positions are shown by the arrows on the photograph.

Equalising three points with a single sling

Let us consider a poorly equipped bolted mountain route. The stances may have gear on, but the pitches may require the traditional placing of gear on the lead. The stances are furnished with two unconnected bolts, but their placement looks a bit dodgy. As you have a rack available, you decide to back them up by placing a good wire nearby. Should you wish to operate

the belay from one point, you need to bring these three anchors together. This can be done with a long sling; a 240cm (16-foot) one would be ideal.

- Clip the sling into each of the three anchor points.
- Hold onto the sections of sling from between the anchors and pull them downwards so that you end up with the sling pulled into three loops in the direction of loading.
- Making sure all the loops are the same length, tie an overhand knot in them. This creates the attachment point, from which you can belay.

Tip

The sewn section of the sling will almost always find its way to where it is not wanted, either as part of the knot or running across a karabiner. Take a moment before tying any of the equalising knots above to ensure that the seam is out of the way and will not become incorporated into any part of the system.

BELAYING

There are many considerations when setting up a belay system, such as whether to use a direct or semi-direct system, the angles relevant to the ABC (see below) and the positioning of the belayer, and these are examined in the following pages. To be able to belay effectively and safely is obviously a primary skill, but it requires a bit more thought than simply clipping the rope into a belay device.

ABC

A = anchor
B = belayer
C = climber

The ABC of climbing is a fundamental check that you should carry out each time you are preparing to belay, whether at the bottom or top of a route. It is really only relevant to semi-direct belays, but would be a good check to run through whatever system you are setting up.

It is essential that all three components are tight and in line. If you, as belayer (B), are slack on the anchor (A) and the climber should fall you will be pulled forwards and possibly get injured or let go of the rope. If the climber (C) is not in a direct line with the belayer (B) and anchor (A), then you, as belayer, will be pulled to one side when loaded, again risking injury.

Make it a habit to always think about ABC and you won't go far wrong.

TYPES OF BELAY

Belaying, the control of the rope to safeguard a climber, is a fundamental skill that must be learned and understood.

As far as most types of technical sport climbs are concerned, there are two relevant types of belay: direct and semi-direct. These are different in character and in application, and each has its place in a climber's arsenal. The skill is to know when one will be more appropriate than the other, and to be able to use it in the correct manner. The differences between the two types are as follows:

- **Direct belay** The entire load created by holding the weight of a falling climber is held directly by the anchor system, with the belayer not being affected at all. This may take the form of an Italian hitch directly onto a screwgate clipped to a bolt or chain, or a device such as a Grigri or SUM (see page 47) being used in a similar manner.

- **Semi-direct belay** The belayer uses a standard belay device or a Grigri or SUM belay device clipped into their harness tie-in loop. Part of the load is directed through to the anchor (if used – see ground anchors

4

later in this chapter) and part is taken by the belayer. A semi-direct belay is most commonly used when safeguarding a leader.

Both methods have advantages and disadvantages, the most pertinent of which are outlined below.

DIRECT BELAY

Advantages	Disadvantages
• Easy to set up if anchor in place.	• Requires a totally solid anchor.
• Belayer out of the system, thus does not get pulled around in the event of a fall.	• Inappropriate for belaying a leader under some situations, such as when a spike anchor is used.
• For bringing up a second on a multi-pitch route, the device can be behind belayer, protecting the second well onto the stance.	• Having brought up a second on a multi-pitch route, the system may have to be converted to semi-direct in order to belay the leader on the next pitch.
• Belayer can escape the system easily, to render emergency assistance if necessary.	• The direction of feed of rope is constant, possibly getting in climber's way during sections of route, particularly if bottom-roping.
	• Belayer on a high stance needs to remember own security and clip into anchor with cow's-tail or similar.

SEMI-DIRECT BELAY

Advantages	Disadvantages
• Easy to clip device straight into harness or tie-in loop.	• Belayer part of system thus pulled around when holding a fall.
• Easy to give direct assistance when bottom-roping.	• Time-consuming for belayer to escape system if needed in an emergency.
• Possibility of giving a 'dynamic' belay and braking effect to leader.	• Ground anchors may be needed depending upon style of route being climbed.
• No special anchor system needed.	• Belayer on a high stance needs to be well anchored and in suitable position from which to take load should climber slip.
• If no ground anchor being used, belayer can move around base of crag, terrain permitting, to keep rope out of climber's way.	

In practical terms there is little to choose between the two methods. Apart from the obvious factors – such as the provision of a bomb-proof anchor should a direct belay be chosen – much will depend on the choice of the party given local conditions.

DIRECT BELAY

It is essential that the equipment – such as a chain or single ring-bolt – used to clip the direct belay system into is solid beyond question. Failure of this part of the anchor will result in the entire system falling apart, with dire consequences. Having said that, a solid direct belay is a good way to manage the rope, allowing some degree of freedom for the belayer.

Direct belays may be used on the ground or, more frequently, from above to protect a second. Ground anchors suitable for direct belays may be provided, such as a bolt in a handy boulder, or can be constructed by the team with a sling around an appropriately placed tree or similar.

Using a passive belay device
Although it is possible to use this on a direct belay it is rarely seen, and the difficulty of controlling the system often means that other procedures are chosen instead. If you do elect to use a passive device you must ensure that you are positioned in a suitable place from which to operate it, bearing in mind the critical importance of the braking position needed by the dead rope. As direct anchors often lend themselves to the belayer being in front of the attachment point, either an active device, a passive self-locking device or an Italian hitch may be found to be easier to operate.

Using an active belay device
If an active device – such as a Grigri or SUM – is being used, it is essential that the camming system and moving parts of the unit will not be compromised by touching the rock or any other projection near the anchor. If the locking mechanism is hindered in any

Passive belay device on a direct belay

Active belay device on a direct belay

4

BASIC SKILLS

way, the result may be that the climber simply free-falls to the ground, or at least the length of the rope. A quick tug-check when the system is set up will confirm that all is well – remember to pull the live rope (the one from the climber) in the direction of loading, and look to see if the unit is anywhere near an obstruction. If it is, either extend the anchor or choose a different belay system.

Using an Italian hitch
This is a useful way of belaying, and is perfectly suited to a direct anchor system. Make sure that there are no twists between the live and dead ropes, as this may make taking in and paying out confusing. The hitch may tend to twist the rope a little after time, but letting the rope hang free or simply chasing any twists out to the end between routes will do the trick.

Italian hitch on a direct belay

Using a passive self-locking belay device
This device is well suited for use on direct belays, but with one very important proviso – it is extremely difficult to pay rope through it when under load. As long as the climber can get his weight off the rope then slack can be paid out. If the climber cannot get his weight off the rope – as when hanging free under an overhang or bulge – it is extremely difficult to release it under load. See below for information on how to release the load in this situation.

Passive self-locking belay device on a direct belay

Releasing a passive self-locking belay device under load
If the worst comes to the worst and the device is locked, with your second unable to get his weight off the rope, you need to use a technical system to solve the problem.

1   Once the device has come under load, the dead rope is taken to a belay device on the harness of the belayer. If nothing else is to hand, this could be an Italian hitch, locked off while you work.

2 A sling is threaded though the kara-biner at the back of the locked-off device, either doubled or secured with a lark's-foot.

3 This sling is now taken up and through a suitable point on the belay system, per-haps made by clipping a karabiner into the chain or one of the anchor bolts.

4 It is then brought back down to the belayer and clipped into his harness, and adjusted to be snug, preferably with an overhand knot.

5 The belayer, holding onto the dead rope coming from the belay device on his harness, commits all his weight to the sling, which has the effect of mov-ing the rear lock-off karabiner up and releasing the jammed rope.

6 The belayer now controls the descent of the climber with the device on the belayer's harness.

Releasing set-up for a locked-off passive self-locking device

To abseil loop of belayer

To abseil loop of belayer

To climber

Considerations

It is important to think about the conse-quences of using a direct belay system to safeguard a leader. In some situations this may be appropriate, but in others it could cause a pull on the anchor in an unwel-come direction, making holding a fall very awkward indeed.

For instance, if a direct belay has been set up using an active belay device clipped into a chain on a multi-pitch stance, and it is then used to belay the leader as he con-tinues on and up, the effect of a fall may be to pull the device upside down, forcing the locking arm against the rock and stopping it from braking effectively. In many multi-pitch situations, therefore, a mixture of the two techniques will often be used. A direct belay will be deployed for bringing up the second to the stance, then the rope system will be swapped over and a semi-direct sys-tem used for the leader. This allows good control of the rope and the bodyweight of the belayer, connected to the anchor, helps counter any problems in the event of a fall.

SEMI-DIRECT BELAY

This style of belaying can be accomplished with either an active or passive belay device. There is little to choose between them, and the final decision will often depend on what equipment is available.

The attachment of the device to the harness must be done with a screwgate karabiner in order to provide maximum security. Most harnesses are designed with a small sewn loop at the front, sometimes called a 'belay loop' but more accurately referred to as an 'abseil loop'. The belay device is often clipped into this loop.

Each harness manufacturer supplies instructions with their product, and you should read this information carefully. There has been a bit of debate in recent years over whether the abseil loop is designed to take a shock-loading. As sewn tape, it is an extremely strong point and can easily handle the weight of a climber, either

Belay device clipped into the abseil loop

Belay device clipped into the rope tie-in loop

when abseiling or when bottom-roping a route. However, if shock-loading is to occur – as in the event of a leader fall – the tape loop does not have any shock-absorbing properties. Check your harness instructions to see if the manufacturer recommends belaying a leader from this loop or not. To avoid this problem tie into the end of the rope and belay from the resulting rope tie-in loop. This has the advantage that the loop – made from the climbing rope – has dynamic properties and directs a lot of the force of a fall away from the harness.

Note

Wherever you belay from, take a moment when clipping the belay device in to check that the rope is running through in the correct manner and is not twisted. If you are belaying a leader or controlling a bottom rope, the 'live' rope (the one from the climber) should go into the top of the device and emerge from the bottom of it, being then held by your controlling hand (and known as the 'dead' rope). This will ensure that there are no twists in the rope, which could otherwise result in jerky paying out of the rope, or even the rope jamming in the device in the event of a fall.

GROUND ANCHORS

Ground anchors – used to anchor the belayer in place – are most often used on single-pitch routes. On multi-pitch climbs the climbers tend to be anchored by default, thus protected for both downwards and upwards pulls. The use of a ground anchor on a single-pitch route helps to prevent the belayer being pulled upwards and inwards in the event of the leader taking a fall, protecting both the belayer and the leader.

Tests have shown that a belayer who is pulled 1m upwards before coming tight on their anchor when holding a fall will reduce the impact force on the running belay and anchor system at the optimum level of shock absorbency. However, in most cases the belayer will secure himself snugly to the anchor, as this seems to be the safest and most comfortable way to control the rope. How the belayer uses a ground anchor is down to personal choice, and it should be remembered that we are most often dealing with securely placed bolts as running belays, where it could be argued that there is little chance of them being detrimentally affected by the forces caused by a leader fall. This is not always the case, and great care should be taken when reducing the shock-absorbing properties of the ground anchor, should one be used.

Think about the following before deciding whether or not you need a ground anchor:

- Do you need one? You may be at a crag and notice that no one else is arranging a ground anchor, but does that mean that you don't need to?
- Are you considerably heavier or lighter than the person you are belaying?
- Are the bolts spaced a long way apart?
- Is the leader climbing at the top of his grade and, as such, likely to take a fall?
- Is there anything nearby that could cause injury should you be pulled forwards and upwards in the event of a fall, such as a projecting block or tree branch?
- Is the ground on which you are standing uneven – could you slip and pull the leader off?
- Is it possible to arrange a ground anchor? A sport route above a shingle beach with a high first bolt and no low bolted anchor provision will make the construction of a ground anchor difficult, whereas other crags may offer a profusion of low anchors such as nearby trees or boulders, or purpose-placed bolts into which the belayer can clip.

Ground anchor positions

Remember: just because others at the crag may not be using ground anchors it doesn't mean that you shouldn't! If you do feel that an anchor should be constructed, think about where support should best come from. Consider these three positions (listed in order of preference):

- **From behind** This may be possible by using a tree trunk, root, boulder or other natural feature. There may be ground anchors already in place, such as a bolt placed in a large boulder, or secured to the bedrock.

- **From low down in front** Some crags have bolts positioned very low down, almost at foot level, for use as ground anchors. Alternatively, a piece of placed gear, such as a wire, will do the job.

- **From around shoulder height in front** This will often necessitate the placing of a piece of protection into which the belayer can clip. This anchor – although less efficient for taking an upwards pull – is preferable should the ground be uneven and the belayer be at risk of slipping and tugging the leader off. To hold a leader fall, the belayer can sit back on the placement and use his bodyweight to hold the fall.

Ground anchor attachments

A ground anchor may be used when either leading or bottom-roping a route. A heavy climber could just as easily pull a lighter belayer off their feet when falling from a bottom-roped route as when leading it. The attachment from the belayer to the anchor needs to be considered, and a couple of important points noted.

- If the belayer were holding a leader, it would be best if he were attached to the anchor by means of the rope. This ensures that all parts of the system have shock-absorbing properties and any load on the system is reduced in the event of a fall.
- If the belayer is watching out for a climber on a bottom-rope system, he may choose to clip into the anchor

Belaying with the rope to a ground anchor behind	Belaying with a sling to the ground anchor bolt	Belaying with a ground anchor to the front

with a sling. A sling will not stretch, thus absorbing load, so is not first choice for holding a leader fall. However, in the case of bottom-roping there is little chance of the rope being shock-loaded as any fall will result in a simple dangle. The anchor will not be loaded to any great extent, the stretch of the climbing rope dealing with any forces involved.

To sum up: if belaying a leader tie onto the anchor with a rope, if belaying a second a sling will do the job adequately.

ROPE MANAGEMENT

This is an important skill to acquire, as being unable to sort the rope properly may result in knots and twists which would be hard to get rid of when concentrating on belaying a leader. Efficient management of the rope starts with how you keep the rope for storage and transportation. If the rope has been coiled, for example, there is a good chance that twists will occur.

The following three ways of storing and carrying a rope are recommended.

Flaking

This allows the rope to sit as it likes, but as there are no twists introduced when packing the rope away it will undo easily without kinks. Flake the rope from the middle first one way

Note
....
On multi-pitch routes great care needs to be exercised to ensure that there are no tangles. Consideration should be given to how the rope will be running if the second will be leading through, or if just one person will be leading the entire route. On hanging stances, flaking the rope (see below) across the belay rope or cow's-tail will help keep things tidy. Alternatively, commercially available 'rope tidies' can be used, into which the rope is flaked to keep it out of harm's way.

4

BASIC SKILLS

FLAKING A ROPE

STEP 1 Start flaking the rope by laying lap coils across your hand.

STEP 2 Wrap a few turns of rope around the coils.

STEP 3 Pull a loop through the top and place this over all the coils, pulling the ends tight.

STEP 4 The completed flaked rope will not kink or knot when uncoiled.

(Opposite)
Using a rope mat keeps dirt and debris out of the system

Tip

Make sure that you do not bury the ends under piles of coils when getting the rope ready for use, whatever deployment method you use. If running it through, lay the first end off to one side, pile the rope nearby, then place the other end near the first. The leader will tie onto the rope coming from the top of the pile, the belayer or second attaches to the end coming from the bottom of the pile.

then the other across your hand. When there are a couple of metres left, wrap a few turns around the flakes. Pass a loop through the top and pull this over and round, tugging the ends to tighten it. To deploy the rope, lift off the final loop, unwrap the coils, place the rope on the ground and run it through to make sure that there are no knots. Providing it has been correctly flaked in the first place there won't be any.

Snaking

This can be done with the rope single, doubled or tripled. It makes for a slightly bulky carry, but the rope will undo very easily with no twisting. Having tied a loop in the end of the rope, pull through a short section. Put your hand through this and pull through another, repeat the process until you come to the end, and tie it off. To uncoil the rope for use, undo the last knot and pull – the rope will snake its way free and only leave you with one final knot to untie.

Using a rope bag

Undoubtedly the best method for sport routes is to use a rope bag or mat. This is a large sheet of waterproof material, about 1.5 x 2m square, which folds away into a small rucksack, often attached. The climbing rope is attached to a tab at one corner, fed into a heap in the middle, and the other end tied to a second tab before the whole lot is rolled away

SNAKING A ROPE

STEP 1 Having either doubled or trebled the rope, tie a loop in it.

STEP 2 Pull a series of loops through each other, working your way along the length of the rope. At the end, tie a knot to lock off the loops.

STEP 3 The rope can now be carried in a rucksack or rope bag, and will not tangle when unravelled.

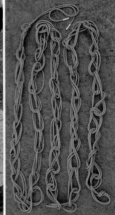

Tip

Before uncoiling the rope, think about where the belayer will be standing, whether ground anchors will be used, and if he is left- or right-handed. These factors will all make a difference as to where you place the rope on the ground. Being tidy at this stage will go a long way to prevent problems later on.

into the rucksack for carrying. Before use the mat is spread out on the ground, the top end of the rope unfastened and the leader ties directly onto it.

SINGLE, TWIN- AND DOUBLE-ROPE TECHNIQUES

Climbing with two ropes – using double- or twin-rope techniques – brings its own set of challenges as far as rope management is concerned. This is particularly so with multi-pitch routes. It is often best if just one rope is used for attachment to the anchor, and care taken that the ropes are run through at an equal speed. If the same person is to lead the entire route the ropes need to be 'turned round' at the end of each pitch. This can be done when the second person arrives at the stance, each running a rope through at the same pace, until the ropes to the leader are coming from the top of the piles.

Single-roping

Most often you will be climbing using a single rope. This is quick, simple, safe and lightweight and is how routes are completed the world over.

Multi-pitch routes that do require long abseils to get down will most often be noted in the guidebook. Even then, a team may still choose to stick with a standard single-rope ascent, either towing or carrying up another rope, often on the back of the second climber, to facilitate the abseil descent.

Twin-roping

This method is used where two very thin and light ropes are deployed and treated as one. They are both clipped into each karabiner and often used in tandem on the anchor. Although this style of climbing is losing popularity on short single-pitch routes, it can often be seen on long pitches and mountain routes. The advantage is that the team has a full distance – say 60m – abseil length, as the ropes can be used to their full extent. It also means that, should a rope become damaged through rock fall, there will be a replacement rope.

One problem with the twin-rope method is the placing of both ropes into each of the karabiners on runners. In the event of a fall the rope nearer the back bar of the karabiner is squeezed slightly by the outer one, which will move slightly faster, thus generating heat, which is undesirable. Also, with the advent of modern-day lightweight karabiners, having a wide load at the base of the krab can exert an unwanted levering effect on it. This is made much worse if the karabiner is vibrating as the rope runs through it during the fall, as the krab can be stretched with the gate open, causing a massive reduction in its strength.

Double-roping

This is often confused with twin-roping. Double-roping is a far more popular method, albeit with the ropes being handled in a different manner.

- Only one rope is clipped into each runner. This avoids any problem with incorrectly loading the karabiner.
- This allows the leader to make a clip to a higher runner whilst still being protected from a lower one. If a single rope was being used and the leader slipped while making the clip, he would fall a lot further. With traditionally placed gear, using double ropes also means that rope drag – caused by the rope zigzagging between placements – can be dramatically reduced. This is not usually a problem on sport routes, however, as the bolts normally follow a fairly straight line.
- There is also the ability to abseil a full-rope length, as with twin-roping.

4

BASIC SKILLS

The disadvantages of double-roping are the extra care needed to belay properly, as two ropes are running through the belay device (an active device such as a Grigri is unusable as it only deals with a single rope), and the extra weight involved.

Although the vast majority of sport climbs would be completed using a single rope, a double-rope system may be useful in a couple of instances when dealing with poorly equipped multi-pitch routes, as these may have the stances equipped with chains, but not be bolted on any of the pitches. In this case:

- Double roping would ease the clipping of leader-placed protection, such as wires and cams, allowing for a safe and smooth running of each pitch.
- As many multi-pitch routes require the team to abseil off to finish, double 60m ropes would greatly increase the speed of the descent. Twin-roping would also be appropriate here.

TYING ONTO ANCHORS

In many cases it will be necessary to tie onto an anchor in one of the following positions:

- Ground anchor
- Anchor set up at a stance on a multi-pitch route
- Anchor set up at the very top of a climb.

In many cases, tying on will entail connecting the belayer to the anchor system by using either a cow's-tail or the rope. Although a cow's-tail is a very useful tool and is swift to deploy, using the rope will sometimes be the only option, particularly if a semi-direct belay is to be used to safeguard a leader.

When tying onto the anchor with the intention of using it for a semi-direct belay, it is important to ensure that the belayer has followed the ABC (anchor–belayer–climber)

rule and is not only tight onto the anchor but also in line. If not he runs the risk of being pulled sideways or forwards in the event of a leader fall, possibly resulting in loss of control of the rope or injury.

Cow's-tail

This is a common way of connecting a climber or belayer to an appropriate part of the system. It is very useful when leading routes as the cow's-tail, attached to the leader's harness, can be quickly deployed when the lower-off has been reached, thus protecting him whilst he arranges the rope for descent.

In its simplest form – which is often the best – a cow's-tail will consist of a short 60cm sling connected to the harness with a lark's-foot. This connection can be made either around the abseil loop or around the leg loops and waist belt, following the line of the climbing rope. The sling is furnished with a screwgate karabiner, which is clipped to one of the gear loops on the harness to keep everything neat and tidy.

Clipped into an anchor with a cow's-tail attached to the harness

When needed, the screwgate is taken off the harness and clipped into wherever is appropriate, for instance into the chain on a lower-off. Remember that the sleeve of the screwgate needs to be done up to prevent accidental opening.

Tip

Before leading up a route, check that your extenders are hanging outside the cow's-tail so that there is little chance of them snagging when you take one off to use on a bolt.

Some cow's-tails will be made from a single length of rope, one end tied around the harness and the other with a loop in to take a screwgate karabiner. Others may be constructed from a sling that has (commercially) sewn loops running along it, enabling the user to vary his distance from the anchor.

Note

Whichever method is chosen, it is important that the climber ends up the correct distance from the anchor, and is in no danger of slipping away from it and being unable to regain a footing and thus the anchor itself.

Remember that the sling is made from non shock-absorbent material and – although very strong when loaded statically – will transmit high forces to the anchor if it is used as a connection for holding a leader fall. Only use slings where the load will be static, such as when clipping lower-offs, when belaying on a bottom-rope system and so on.

Tying on to one anchor point in reach with a clove hitch

Tying on with the rope

In many cases it will be a good idea to have the rope as part of the anchor system. This is often unavoidable on multi-pitch routes, but may also be useful on ground anchors and the like. A clove hitch is a good solution for clipping into a single anchor point where you can reach the karabiner.

This knot locks off under load but is very easy to adjust, allowing you to fine-tune the position at which you are going to stand or sit. It is because of this useful aspect that I mentioned being able to reach the karabiner into which it is clipped. If that karabiner was out of reach you would spend a lot of time going backwards and forwards trying to get the tension right. If that is the case, and the anchor karabiner is a little distance away, a better knot would be the figure of eight on the bight. This knot is tied at the harness, thus always remaining within reach. It is quick to tie and very strong, and should be practised until it can be tied efficiently.

(Left) **Tying back to the harness with a figure of eight on the bight**

(Below left) **Tied onto one anchor with a clove hitch at the harness**

A second method, when dealing with a single anchor point out of reach, is to use a clove hitch but this time to connect it to a screwgate karabiner on your harness. This means that the hitch is always right there and easy to adjust. However, you may prefer not to clutter up the harness with a second karabiner and still opt for the figure of eight method.

Tying into two anchors

Sometimes you may be faced with having two anchor points to tie into, perhaps two separate bolts at a stance, or using a piece of leader-placed protection to back up an existing anchor system. Whatever the reason, the basic rule stays the same: if the anchors are in reach, clove hitches are fine; if out of reach then use figure of eights on the bight.

- **Two anchor points within reach** With the rope from the harness, go to one anchor point first and clip in with a clove hitch. Adjust this so that you are snug. Leave a little slack and go to the second anchor, again clipping in with a clove hitch. From here, come back down to your harness and tie in with a figure of eight on the bight. If this final length of rope ends up a little bit loose it does not matter; the clove hitch on the anchor can be used to tighten it.

(Right) **Tying onto two anchor points within reach with two clove hitches and a figure of eight on the bight**

(Below right) **Tying onto two anchor points out of reach with two figure of eights on the bight**

- **Two anchor points out of reach** Use a figure of eight on the bight for each of them. The quickest way to arrange this will be to clip into both, then get yourself to your stance while pulling down on the rope from between the anchors. Now tie on with figure of eights, starting with the rope from the first anchor, then the second.

It is important that sections of rope going to the two anchors are tied so that they are sharing the load, otherwise the anchors hold the weight unequally which could cause problems if the placements are less than perfect.

Although it may seem like a good idea to do a similar thing as with a single anchor out of reach (tying a clove hitch into a karabiner at the harness) this is not a good solution when coming back from two anchors. The clove hitches would be very difficult to adjust, and this could also result in the karabiner being loaded a long way from the strong point at the base of the back bar, causing a levering effect on the gate.

4

BASIC SKILLS

SPORT CLIMBING   61

Multiple anchors

Once you have mastered the idea of using clove hitches and figure of eights, there is no limit to the ways in which you can tie onto one, two, three or more anchors. A clove hitch and a figure of eight can even be used in conjunction, such as where one anchor point is in reach and the other out of reach. Go to the furthest one first and come back to your harness with a figure of eight on the bight. The rope coming out of this knot can then go to the nearer anchor with a clove hitch, with no other knots required.

Tying onto one anchor in reach, the other out of reach

BOTTOM-ROPING

Delicate slab climbing, Portland

5 BOTTOM-ROPING

(Opposite)
The author being lowered
after leading a steep route.
The belayer is in a good,
braced position.

Bottom-roping is a method of climbing where the belayer is positioned and controls the rope from the bottom of the route, with the rope running up through a highpoint and back down to the climber. This is often incorrectly called 'top-roping', but as the name implies this involves the belayer being positioned at the top of the route and controlling things from there. Top-roping is quite common on traditional rock climbs, where the climbing team can top-out and walk off. However, as the majority of sport climbs finish either just below, or quite some distance from, the top, belaying from above is not usually an option.

Bottom-roping is very common on sport routes, and this will often be the method by which the second person ascends. The first climber will have led the route, arranged the lower-off appropriately and come down to the ground. The rope is then left in place and the pair swaps over, with the second climber now protected by the rope from above.

This technique allows routes to be climbed in relative safety, especially if you are trying to climb something a grade or two harder than you have previously attempted. A slip will just result in a dangle on the rope and not in an actual fall of any distance (as long as your belayer is paying attention!).

SETTING UP A BOTTOM-ROPING SESSION

This takes a bit of planning, as it may not be as easy as it first seems to get a rope rigged through the lower-off point. If one of your team is going to lead the route things are more straightforward. The leader makes his way up, clipping extenders as usual, and lowers off once he has come up with a suitable rigging system at the lower-off point. However, if no one is keen to lead the route – usually because you are going to try something above your normal leading grade – you still have some other options.

Accessing the lower-off from above

Although reaching down from above to reach the lower-off may sometimes be an option, it is not ideal, and you should take great care when doing so. There may be loose debris at the top of the crag that you could inadvertently knock down onto parties below. Also, as lower-offs will almost

always be on vertical ground just below the cliff top, take extreme care when leaning over to clip them or thread the rope through. It would be all too easy to over-reach, slip and fall the height of the cliff.

In practice this is often out of the question as many sport routes have their lower-offs some way below the top of the crag. This means that the last part of the route avoids areas of vegetated or loose ground, or where the grade of the climb would be radically altered, either far easier or harder than what has gone before.

Unless you can be absolutely sure that this technique is going to be safe, it's far more sensible to either come up with a different plan for the climbing session, or set up a safety line. You could use a couple of slings clipped around a convenient tree, connected to your harness with your cow's-tail or a separate screwgate. Although you are unlikely to have a spare rope, you can still safeguard yourself using the rope you are going to climb with.

The following procedure should be followed, assuming that there is a reasonable tree (or suitable boulder) a few metres back from the edge of the crag – as a strong attachment point for the rope – and that the lower-off is a simple ring and chain rig, supported by two bolts.

1 Place a sling and screwgate karabiner around the tree.
2 Tie a figure of eight on the bight in the end of the rope and clip this into the screwgate, doing it up. If a sling is not available, tie the rope around the tree using a figure of eight rewoven or a bowline.
3 Clip a screwgate karabiner into the abseil loop on your harness.
4 Estimate how much rope is needed to get you safely to the edge of the cliff, and tie a clove hitch in it, clipping this to your harness. Get to the edge of the cliff at a suitable point to rig the lower-off. The clove hitch allows for adjustment of the tension between you and the tree anchor.
5 Thread the end of the climbing rope through the lower-off and lower it to the ground. Allow a couple of metres of extra slack to ensure that the end is still in reach once it has all been rigged.
6 Holding the two sections of rope together below the bolt, get back onto safe ground, bringing the rope with you.
7 Untie the clove hitch and anchor knot and throw all the rope down the line of the route.
8 Let go of the two ropes in your hand, which will follow the rest over the edge. The bottom rope is now rigged.

Abseiling to rig

It may be possible to abseil to the lower-off and rig from there, continuing the abseil once the bottom rope has been set up. This will obviously require the use of a second rope and somewhere from which to rig it. You should protect yourself during the descent (see Chapter 10), plus consider making yourself more secure when you are at the lower-off working with the bottom rope. The simplest method here would be to take a few wraps of the abseil rope around your thigh, which would help to back-up the French prusik safety system. As before, consider the hazards associated with abseiling to rig, not least the possibility of loose rock and other climbers below.

Using a clip stick

If you do not want to lead the route prior to arranging the bottom rope – perhaps it is very hard and you want the exercise without the stress of leading – you may be able to use a clip stick to get to the lower-off. This is akin to the red-point style of ascent, except that you will not be leading the route after practising it. If your stick is long enough not every bolt will need to be clipped and you could bypass every other one. However, you may still wish to clip the empty bolts as you hoist yourself past to the next one, for added security. To get to the highpoint using a clip stick use the following method:

1   Tie onto the climbing rope and have your partner put you on belay.
2   Put a bight of rope into an extender and, using the clip stick, reach up and clip the highest bolt you can, pulling the stick down afterwards.
3   Either climb up on a tight rope or, if the ground is very awkward, 'yard' up by pulling down on the rope running to your belayer.

Tip
· · · · · · · · · · · · · · · · · · ·
It may be possible to use a clip stick from the top to reach the lower-off. It should be used with a screwgate karabiner for security, and this can be backed up when the first climber reaches the chain. To stop the weight of the rope pulling the karabiner off the end of the stick, try holding onto a bight of rope until the lower-off is clipped. If this does not work, clip a long sling into the climbing rope and use this to support it. The sling can be retrieved once connection with the lower-off has been made.

5

BOTTOM-ROPING

4 When you arrive at the bolt, clip yourself in using a short cow's-tail and let it hold your weight. Ensure that you are placing a downwards, rather than outwards, pull on the bolt, as it will be stronger in this direction.

5 You can have your belayer pass the clip stick up to you. Better still, some designs have a loop that enables it to be carried on your harness. Use the stick to reach up and clip an extender and rope into a higher bolt.

6 Have your belayer take you in tight, unclip the cow's-tail, and climb or yard up to the next highpoint.

7 Clip the cow's-tail in and repeat the process as often as is needed to reach the lower-off point. This will also have to be clipped from below using the stick, unless there is a bolt situated right next to it.

8 Clip yourself into the lower-off with the cow's-tail and arrange the rope as appropriate, usually following the same procedure as when lowering off after leading.

9 However, it may be necessary to use a sling to rig the lower-off and make it suitable for bottom-roping if it consists of two separate bolts or staples.

OVERHANGING ROUTES

You may have elected to bottom-rope a route as you want to try something far harder than you feel like leading. It may be that the route is overhanging for some or all of its distance, or there might be a move or two below a roof or bulge. If the rope is hanging some distance away from the rock for all or part of the route, this needs to be taken into account when rigging. As you are being lowered back down to the ground after setting up at the lower-off, use extenders to clip into runners at suitable points on the route in order to keep the rope close to the rock. Not all the bolts would have to be clipped, just the key ones that will keep the rope in a line parallel to

Clipping the lower-off with a clip stick when setting up a bottom rope

the rock. There are two main reasons for doing this:

• If the climber needs the rope to be taken in tight for some assistance on a move, there is a chance that he could be pulled off as the rope will be running over his shoulder and away unless it is held close to the rock.

• Should the climber fall or sit on the rope for a rest, he will have little chance of regaining the rock as he could be hanging some distance out from it. Keeping the rope close to the rock will also prevent him from swinging out from the route where an obstruction behind him – a tree or other section of crag – could cause injury.

As the climber makes his way up, he will have to take the rope out of the extenders as he reaches them, otherwise he will be unable to progress any higher. If he is the last to go, he can remove the entire extender once it has done its job of keeping the rope in close, and be lowered straight down from the top after he has completed the route.

If there are others trying the climb they will need to re-clip the extenders, which could have been left hanging on the bolts, while they descend. This may, in certain places, require the climber to swing out from the rock by pushing off with the feet, and grabbing the extender as he swings back, in order that the clip can be made. Take care if doing this: if you are any distance away from the rock you will have to hold on tight to the extender in order to

Take care not to let your hand slip if grabbing an extender when swinging out

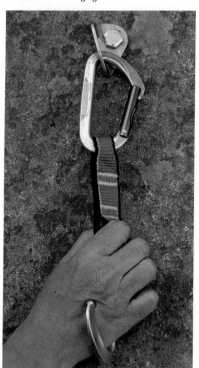

stop the swing, and stay there for a couple of seconds while you clip the rope in. It is quite possible to slip out a little due to momentum after grasping the extender. As your hand slides down the tape the karabiner at the rope end pinches itself around your hand, holding you fast. This is extremely painful; the nose of the karabiner digs into the small bones on the back of your hand while your bodyweight tries to swing you out further. In some cases this has been exacerbated by the belayer, either panicking or misreading the situation, lowering the poor climber some more so that his weight is then hanging from the karabiner jammed around his hand.

TYPES OF BOTTOM-ROPE RIGGING AT THE LOWER-OFF

Chain with single ring

There are two common set-ups at the top of routes: single-point lower-offs and double-point lower-offs.

Single point will normally be the easiest to rig and operate, as it often only requires the rope to be threaded through the ring and thence back down to the ground. This is exactly the system used when lowering off after leading the climb, which will be how most parties will be working. If, however, the ring through which the rope is to be passed is very thin – say less than 8mm – or shows signs of ageing and deterioration, it would be a good idea to use a screwgate karabiner, or even two, in its place. You will have to make this decision, taking into account the state of the ring, the severity of the climb and the length of time or number of people that are going to be using the rope.

For instance, you may have noticed that the ring is a bit thin and a little rusty. You have two friends who wish to try the route, but you think it may be a bit hard for them. In this situation equipping the lower-off with screwgates would be a good idea, as the route may be in use for some time

Running the rope through a maillon or ring on a chain. There should be no possibility that the rope will be damaged if choosing this method.

A single screwgate could be used to provide connection to a lower-off chain

Using two screwgates clipped into the chain to ensure each part of the system is loaded equally

and the rope will certainly be running over the belay point a number of times, often under tension. Alternatively, on the same route and lower-off ring but with a competent partner who just wants a bit of exercise but doesn't want to lead you may decide to thread through as normal and save having to re-climb the route to de-rig kit.

Note

Bear in mind that the rope will be under tension at least some of the time, even if it is just during a lower, and that it can become damaged by poor or ageing equipment. As the rope is your lifeline – and also a very expensive piece of kit – you may decide to err on the side of caution and rig your own system

Rigging your own system

If you elect to bypass the ring and rig your own system, using just one screwgate is fine. Rig it so that the gate opens out from the rock and the opening is at the bottom to prevent the problem of 'gate creep'. When a rope is run through a karabiner – particularly under tension such as when lowering a climber – it sets up sufficient vibration to unscrew the locking sleeve of a karabiner. If the screwgate has been rigged with the gate opening at the top and the sleeve unscrews, you will be left with the rope running through the equivalent of a snapgate karabiner, something you should never do. By simply arranging the karabiner with the gate opening at the bottom you solve this problem.

This is why you may sometimes elect to have two screwgates rigged instead of just the one, allowing you to relax in the knowledge that there is no way both would ever undo at the same time. If the chain's hanging position allows, it is best to have the gates opening in opposite directions, one forward and one back, or one left and one right. Make sure that a gate and sleeve cannot contact the rock either during the climb or when under tension lowering; if there is a danger of one doing so, relocate it with the gate away from danger. Having the gate, thus the locking sleeve, rubbing against the rock during a climb could also cause the gate to unscrew. However, gate-opening problems are extremely rare, and with a little forward thinking the session should be trouble-free.

Two independent bolts

Routes that have two bolts or staples as the lower-off need a little more thought as to the best way to rig them.

When descending after leading a route, you will normally be happy with running the rope through both bolts and being lowered off, as that is all the work they have to do – once you are down, you are down, and the rope is pulled through. If you are going to spend time bottom-roping the route you may decide you need to rig a different system which will be kinder to the rope and allow it to run in a smoother manner. This depends on who is climbing and how hard the route is in relation to their ability, as well as the type and state of bolts. If your partner just wants to climb the route as a warm down, and it is well within his capabilities, there should be no problems as long as the bolts at the top allow the rope to pass through smoothly. However, if you plan to spend some time working a route which is hard, and thus expect to have a few falls, or there are several climbers in your group and the rope will need to run over the lower-off bolts a number of times, you may elect to rig a better system at the top.

The basic skill here is being able to equalise anchors (see Chapter 4), which finds its niche with bottom-roping. A 120cm sling will often be the best option, although the distance between the bolts will dictate the final choice. It is unusual, though, to need anything much longer, as the bolts will be placed around 40 or 50cm apart. Any of the equalising methods would be fine. I prefer to clip the sling into both anchors, pull it down from between and tie a figure of eight in it.

Note

Some lower-offs use a single-point style such as a tail-shaped anchor, where the rope is wrapped around the anchor so that the climber can descend in safety. If routes with this style of top bolt are to be climbed as bottom ropes, and used extensively, it may be prudent to back up the top bolt with another safety system. With some designs and styles of twist-and-capture lower-offs it is possible for the rope to creep back over the captive nose, perhaps if it gets flicked or rotates aggressively. A screwgate karabiner clipped into the system is usually all that is needed to prevent this. Alternatively, an extender can be left in place on the last bolt before the top. Climbers can get to this, unclip it and continue. Once they are ready to be lowered back down again and have checked that all is in order, they can descend to the bolt and clip the extender back in. The last person would remove it and be lowered to the ground before the rope is stripped out.

Two anchors equalised with a sling and the rope clipped in with two screwgates in opposition

(*Below left*) **Clip yourself into one of the bolts for security with a cow's-tail**

(*Below centre*) **Equalise the anchors and equip the sling with one or two screwgates**

(*Below right*) **Clip your climbing rope into the screwgates, undo the cow's-tail, and lower off**

Rigging a bottom rope with two independent bolts

Once the sling has been rigged and the isolation knot tied, it can be equipped with a screwgate karabiner, through which the climbing rope will run. Make sure that, as above, it is orientated with the gate away from the rock and the opening at the bottom, in order to avoid gate creep. You may elect to use two screwgates, turned so that the gates face in opposite directions.

So how does the rope get up there in the first place? You will probably have led the route and so will be in a position to thread the rope in front of you. This is obviously a form of the lowering-off style of rigging the rope, but ending up with the result that the rope is clipped through the karabiner on the equalised anchor. To get to this stage, you might wish to adopt the following procedure:

1   Having led the route, clip into one of the top anchors with your cow's-tail.
2   Using a screwgate on each anchor, equalise them using a sling of suitable length.
3   Once you have tied the isolation knot in the sling, clip one (or two) screwgates in, ensuring that the gate is away from the rock and the opening is at the bottom.
4   Clip the climbing rope in and do up the gate/s.
5   Having communicated with your belayer, pull yourself into the anchor and let them take your weight in order to test that all is well with the rig.
6   Unclip the cow's-tail and be lowered to the ground.

This is a very logical progression and quite easy to remember. Always look after your own security when working at height, and ensure that any communication with your belayer is clear and to the point.

Another option is to use two extenders ready furnished with a screwgate on each end. Once you are at the lower-off an extender is clipped into each bolt and the climbing rope run through the resulting two screwgates. This is a quick method, but does not allow for any adjustment as to where the load is taken. For instance, if one bolt is higher than the other – which is very common – all the load of the bottom-roping session will be on this bolt, with the extender from the second one just hanging loose. Although it would serve as a back-up in case the top bolt failed, it would be shock-loaded in the process, possibly causing the failure of the other bolt. However, if the lower-off bolts are side by side, this may be a preferred system to use in some circumstances.

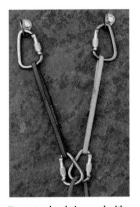

Two extenders being used with screwgate karabiners to share the load

Note

A fairly common sight on bolted crags is the use of two extenders to rig the top section, where two separate bolts are present, in order that others can bottom-rope the route. The leader will climb up and cow's-tail himself into one of the bolts for security while he works. He then clips one extender into each of the bolts and the climbing rope into the two resulting bentgate karabiners. He then unclips the cow's-tail and lowers off. This rig is then used to bottom-rope the other climbers.

Although the set-up is quick, take great care if thinking about using this method. The rope ends up being supported by two snapgate karabiners with no other safeguard. Any untoward movement of the rope, such as caused by the climber being level with the lower-off, or even the oscillation caused when holding a fall, could cause the rope to become disconnected from the system.

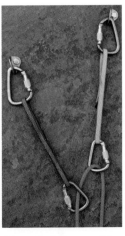

If the anchor bolts are at different heights it would be best to equalise them with a sling, as using two extenders means that one bolt will take all the load

CRAG ETIQUETTE

Certain niceties of crag etiquette should be observed when bottom-roping. Once the bottom rope has been rigged, it would be polite – especially if the crag is busy – to climb the route and then pull the rope down within a reasonable period of time, leaving the climb clear for others. If you have the place to yourselves you can take as long as you like. Do bear in mind that climbers leading a route will always take precedence over those bottom-roping; should other climbers arrive it would be worth checking if the route you are on is the one they are heading for.

Usually – if you have a word with others climbing in the area – they will be fine about working around you. Unfortunately, not everyone who sets up a bottom rope is as considerate, and it is not uncommon to get to a crag and find a number of bottom ropes set up and no one around. This can be extremely irritating, especially if the ropes are on the routes you want to lead and your time is limited. Often, if you start gearing up under the route, someone will appear and you can get things sorted. If no one shows up, even after extensive calling and enquiries, you are left with a dilemma. Do you go off without getting the route under your belt that you had dreamed about and travelled a long way for – or do you pull their ropes through, lead the route with their rope clipped on the back of your harness, and re-rig it at the lower-off so that it is in place for their return? I know what I'd do!

FINISHING THE SESSION

When every member of the team has climbed the route all the gear needs to be stripped out. If you have simply run the rope through the ring at the top, as with a two-bolt-and-chain system, you just need to pull the rope down. However, any gear left up there needs to be retrieved before moving on. Whoever is tasked with the job of getting the gear back will have to decide as to the best way to carry this out, depending on whether it is a single-point or two-bolt anchor.

Single-point lower-off

If it is a single-point lower-off, and you've equipped it with a screwgate or two with the rope running through, retrieval will be very much like the system used for threading a lower-off after a lead.

1   The climber gets to the top and clips himself in with a cow's-tail.
2   He pulls up a bight of the climbing rope and threads it through the ring or suitable point on the anchor.
3   This rope has a figure of eight tied in it, and is then connected to his harness abseil loop with a screwgate karabiner.
4   He unties from the end of the rope and pulls it through.
5   He removes the screwgates from the anchor.
6   Having pulled himself in close and communicated with the belayer, checking the system is OK, he unclips the cow's-tail and is lowered to the ground.

The lower-off system whereby the tail of the rope is passed through the ring with the climber tying back on can also be used.

Equalised two-point lower-off

If the route has a two-point lower-off, and these have been connected with an equalised sling, a slightly different method can be employed:

1 Having gained the lower-off there are a couple of choices. The climber could clip his cow's-tail into one of the bolts and use that as security while he arranges the rope. Alternatively, he could clip a spare screwgate into the equalised sling, next to the one/s being used to run the rope through for the session, and use that as his safety. This has the advantage that his weight is shared by both bolts.

2 He unties from the rope, ensuring that he has clipped it into another point via a knot and karabiner, exactly as for a normal lower, so that it cannot be dropped. The end is passed through and he reties.

3 Pulling into the anchor and communicating with his belayer, he undoes the slings and/or cow's-tail and is lowered to the ground.

Note

Be aware of other users at the crag when you are de-rigging from above, as you are very unlikely to make friends if you start dropping ropes on people. Even if the crag was clear when you started up to the top, others may have arrived and be in close proximity to where you are going to deploy the rope. Have your climbing partner stand at the foot of the route and give you the 'all clear' before throwing the rope down.

Note

Take great care when making your way on foot up to or down from the top of a route. The tops of sport route cliffs are usually infrequently visited, so there may be no decent path for you to follow. As such, there could be a lot of loose rock and overgrowth to negotiate, as well as a turf cornice at the edge of the cliff. Bear in mind also that smooth-soled rock boots have no gripping power whatsoever on grass or mud, so if you are heading cross-country to rig something it would be worthwhile putting on some shoes with more appropriate soles.

CLIPPING NEIGHBOURING LOWER-OFFS

You may wish to spend a while bottom-roping a number of routes, possibly for training purposes or just for fun. Some crags have such closely linked routes that it is possible to reach one lower-off point from another. This opens up the possibility of climbing a number of lines in a short time, as long as you won't be getting in the way of other crag users.

Planning ahead makes things a lot easier in the long run. Let's assume, for convenience, that our ideal crag is equipped with twin bolt lower-offs linked with a chain connected to a ring. In reality, you would most likely get to this point by leading a route, probably the easiest one on your intended series of ticks. If you are intending to bottom-rope from here on in you can connect the climbing rope to the lower-off ring with a screwgate or two and descend from there. The sequence therefore will be as follows.

1 The other climber/s climb the route.
2 When they arrive at the lower-off they are belayed to one side so that they can safely reach the next chain.
3 They clip into it with their cow's-tail to avoid swinging back in the event of a slip.
4 One (or two) screwgate karabiners are clipped into the new ring and the climbing rope connected.
5 They remove their cow's-tail and make their way back to the original lower-off.
6 They take the rope out of here and remove the karabiner/s.
7 They make their way back to the new route and are lowered off.

Note

When talking about lower-offs being close together, anything more than one long arm's span is too far. It is essential that you do not reach out or traverse too far away from the lower-off that is holding you. It may be tempting to do so, but a slip would result in a short and very sharp pendulum back beyond where you started, quite possibly resulting in an injury or, at the least, skin removal as you rattle across the rock. If there is any distance between the lower-offs you would be far safer to come down and either lead the next route or rig the bottom-rope in some other manner.

A CAUTIONARY TALE

The following story is included to show that you can never let your guard down, even when you think you are doing the right thing. However experienced you are something will come up and bite you when you least expect it.

We were climbing at Coupeau, a gneiss crag a short distance out of Chamonix in the French Alps. It's a lovely setting, quite compact and in the trees, ideal for an uncomplicated evening's cragging. Having led a couple of routes, I decided to set up the next two as bottom ropes to wind down. Thus, I found myself at the top of 'Petit Beru' graded at 6b, and then decided to move across to the top of the route next door, called 'Et 1 et 2 et 3/0' at an amenable 6a+. The chain for 'Et 1' was no more than a couple of metres away to my right, so I told Paula what I was going to do and started to move across.

Halfway there I was aware of her calling up to me – something was wrong. Looking down I discovered to my horror that the rope was no longer clipped into the chain at the top of 'Petit Beru' but was hanging down the crag, with nothing between me and the deck except space. So there I was, soloing on dusty 6b ground, pretty tired into the bargain, with a 15m fall in prospect. As my weight was still pushing me right, I had no option but to continue across on small holds with tiny ledges for my feet, making my way towards the next chain. My biggest fear was that Paula would panic and take the rope in, which would have immediately pulled me off the wall and send me crashing to the floor. I managed to get across to the next chain and lock my fingers around it, swinging out at the time, and fumble the rope in to make myself safe again.

So what had happened? I was so involved in the climbing and enjoying the evening I hadn't taken time to think through what I was doing. The chain at the top of 'Petit Beru' was furnished with a steel snapgated captive karabiner, quite a common style today. When I had finished the route, I had clipped into it with the climbing rope running up from the right and through it

The rope unclipping itself from a snaplink lower-off

5

BOTTOM-ROPING

so that it exited to the left and so to my harness. I had then changed my original plan and decided to move across to 'Et 1' in order to set up a bottom rope, and this route was off to the right. Thus the rope ran out of the left-hand side of the steel clip and across the front of the gate as I moved rightwards, which caused it to unclip itself with ease.

Stupidity on my part, as well as not planning ahead properly, were the main causes. Every now and then we need a quick slap to remind us that, however experienced we are, we are still human.

And the moral of this story?

- Firstly, never let your guard drop, even when you are winding down at the end of the day – that's when mistakes creep in.

- Secondly, if you are going to change plans – such as deciding to bottom-rope instead of leading when halfway through the process – think through the consequences and change your technical approach accordingly. If I had decided that I was going to move to the next route before I had clipped the snaplink on the first, I would probably have done it automatically – and correctly – from left to right.

- Finally, back things up. This style of snapgate lower-off is excellent, especially on hard routes, as it allows a quick clip from tired arms and fingers and there is no hanging around. However, it is only designed to take a load straight downwards. If you are going to move around at height – and think carefully before you do – back the snaplink up with a screwgate karabiner so that the rope cannot become detached.

Clip in with a screwgate if using a snaplink lower-off for any period of time

Turbie, near Monaco

6 LEADING

It should be noted that leading, whether on a bolted climb or one where the leader places protection, carries inherent risks. Falling whilst on the lead is dangerous, although it will be treated as part of the deal by climbers who are pushing their grade. Working a route, getting to a highpoint and trying a crux move only to fail and fall is part and parcel of top-grade climbing.

Bolted routes, although they may seem safer with the protection already *in situ*, can present as many hazards to the leader as a traditionally protected route. Z-clipping, stepping through, back-clipping and runner failure are all possibilities, and are discussed later in this chapter. Also consider the actual clipping of a bolt. When arranging leader-placed protection in the rock, there is the opportunity to try a variety of placements and a variety of gear sizes to reach the safest and most workable option. This is based on experience and a continual learning curve. On bolted routes, if there is a bolt in place there is no option but to clip it. You won't know who placed it, when it was put in, how deep it goes or how many falls it has held. Perhaps if it is on a crux move on a popular route, the strength of the rock has been compromised due to having to hold repeated falls. Even with all these unknowns, you still have to clip in and lead on.

Be aware that leading on bolts is not as clinical as some might have you think. However, bolts will *normally* offer a very high degree of protection as long as they have been situated correctly and as long as you clip into them in the correct manner. Being able to clip into a shiny new high-spec ring-bolt set to the side of a scary crux move is one of the greatest feelings in the world, leaving you to concentrate on the climbing safe in the knowledge that failure will result in nothing more than a short flight (and most probably a barracking from watching friends).

HOW TO LEAD A ROUTE

Taking a simple, grade 5, single-pitch sport route of around 15m, this is how the process works:

1   Having selected the route, the climbers prepare the rope, and the leader ties on.

2 The belayer may wish to find a ground anchor. This may be a bolt placed either at the foot of the cliff or a little way behind the belay position, or a handy tree root or similar.

3 The leader ensures that he has the correct number of extenders for the route, plus a couple of extras, as well as any other necessary equipment such as a cow's-tail.

4 Having been placed on belay, the leader starts up the route. The belayer may be spotting the climber at this point, ready to field him should he slip prior to clipping the first bolt.

5 The leader climbs the route and makes himself secure at the lower-off.

6 Following a pre-arranged sequence of calls, the belayer lowers the leader to the ground. Most often, the leader will strip out the extenders as he descends.

7 One of two things may now happen: a) the rope is left in place and the belayer bottom-ropes the route, or b) the rope is pulled through and the belayer turns leader and repeats the above sequence.

Clipping height

The position from which you clip a bolt needs careful consideration. It is very tempting to reach up and clip a bolt as soon as it comes within arm's length, and at times this may be the best place from which to do it. However, think about the amount of rope that is being pulled through the previously clipped extender, in relation to the potential length of fall you could take in the event of a slip at the critical moment just prior to clipping the bolt. If the last clipped extender is around waist level, and the next bolt 1.5m above it, you will end up pulling through around 3m of slack rope. A slip will result in a fall of over 6m, taking into account rope stretch. If, however, you climb up so that the bolt to be clipped is around waist level, and consequently slip, the fall will only be around 3m. The closer you are to the bolt the less drop there is likely to be in the event of a fall.

The psychology of clipping also needs to be considered:

- Even though you are going to fall less far if you are next to the bolt you are clipping into, you may feel safer when clipping from a distance below. This feeling of security, real or otherwise, may also affect your stability – a nervous climber is far more likely to fall than a confident one.

- It may be that the bolt is placed in a position where the better holds are below it, and so clipping from lower down makes more sense.

Clipping high up, increasing possible fall distance

Clipping at waist level, minimising possible fall distance

- If you are level with a clipped bolt it is much easier for your belayer to take the rope in quickly should you need him to, and the security of being by the extender will make you feel a lot happier.

Missing a clip

You may find (or may have already found – this is not restricted to bolted routes) yourself in a situation where the moves above are hard and you elect to clip the next bolt from some distance below. Having placed the extender on tiptoe, you pull through the rope and reach up to clip it. Something makes you bail out at the last moment, perhaps just the thought of the impending fall. You drop the metres of slack rope with a yell of 'No!' to your belayer, who takes the rope in rapidly before you sink, mentally drained, onto the security of the user-friendly extender at your side. I've been there myself, more than once.

Thus, the position from which you clip the bolt is up to you. The most confident climbers will clip the extender at waist height with consummate ease as they seamlessly flow past it onto the next sequence of moves. The vast majority, however, will have to make the call based on personal ability and experience, allied with the uniqueness of each clip and the attendant considerations.

Tip

If clipping into an extender when using a small hold for support, the holding arm may tire very quickly, especially if the route has been hard. As letting go of the hold whilst clipping is not an option, it's worth resting the holding hand for a few seconds. Use the hand that will be doing the clipping to hold you in position whilst you shake out and rest the other arm. When you are ready, swap over and use your newly rejuvenated arm to hold you in position as you make a slick clip with the other.

Note

Once the first bolt has been clipped you may lapse into a false sense of security. If you do not get your positioning right clipping the second bolt can be just as hazardous, but with the potential of a longer fall. If you are some way below the second bolt and pull the rope through, there could be enough slack in the system that – should you slip – a ground fall is a real possibility. Although you may feel that being some way below the bolt is the best option, clipping it as soon as you can reach it, think about the consequences. If you are on a ledge or have a decent handhold, this may be the best place from which to make the clip. However, if the ground is at all technical and you are not confident about your ability to hold on while performing the task, it would be safer to move higher so that the second bolt is between chest and waist height. You will be pulling through the minimum amount of rope and any fall will be a lot shorter than it would be if clipping up from some way below.

Z-clipping

This will sometimes occur when the leader is becoming nervous about moves just made or yet to come. He will not be relaxed and will hold his body close to the rock. If the previous bolt is around waist high, when he reaches down and pulls the rope up he will grab it from below the last bolt. When this bight of rope is clipped in, the rope from the belayer will be running up to the higher bolt, down to the previous one, then up to the leader. This gives rise to two problems.

- The leader is no better protected than he was before clipping, and if he moves up and then falls off he will go some distance.
- Any upward movement will be very difficult as there will be a significant amount of rope drag, making progress virtually impossible.

Z-clipping, which results in rope drag and the potential of a long fall

If the rope is Z-clipped in this way it needs to be sorted out as soon as possible. It will probably be spotted straight away, either by the leader as he tries to move up or by an observant second. To solve it, the rope should be unclipped from the lower bolt. This means that the belayer can take the slack in and the leader will be protected throughout – the lower bolt can be reclipped in the correct place if needed. If the leader, having realised he has Z-clipped, takes the rope out of the top extender, he is again opening himself up to the possibility of a long fall. As the problem may have occurred due to nervousness, having to unclip an extender would do nothing to ease the leader's concerns, so the top bolt is best left clipped in and the lower one undone.

Back-clipping

Back-clipping is where the line taken by the climbing rope is incorrectly introduced into the extender. This is the most frequent mistake made by both beginners and experienced climbers alike. The problem with back-clipping is that, in some circumstances, the rope can undo itself from the extender in the event of a fall. It is also possible for the rope to rotate the extender in such a manner as to allow it to undo from the bolt, again with potentially disastrous consequences. It is essential that the run of the rope, usually dictated by the direction taken by the climber, and the orientation of the karabiner gate, be taken into consideration.

(Right) **Bolt, extender and rope correctly clipped**

(Far right) **An extender back-clipped – something to be avoided**

A bentgate clipped into a bolt; it could unclip when moved by the rope

Bentgate karabiners – the usual choice for the rope end of an extender – are excellent in that the rope can be easily and swiftly placed into them, often with just the slightest push with a finger or thumb, the rest being left up to gravity. However, given the right conditions they can also unclip just as efficiently. The two main rules for correct clipping are that:

• The rope from the belayer to the climber runs up from behind the karabiner and exits from the front, and
• The rope runs across the back bar of the karabiner, with the gate being orientated away from it.

It needs to be clarified from the outset that only the straight gate karabiner on the extender is ever clipped into the bolt. The bentgate karabiner (if one is being used – you may have elected to use two straight gates) is reserved for clipping into the rope. If the bentgate is clipped into a bolt it could undo under certain conditions, such as being rotated by the movement of the rope.

Back-clipping problems

There are three main difficulties associated with back-clipping.

The photograph on the right demonstrates a common mistake on both bolted routes and in traditional climbing, and often results from either hasty clipping or just not thinking through the consequences. The rope to the leader from the belayer has been clipped through from the front of the karabiner, exiting from the back. It is also on the gate side. In the event of a fall, it is possible that the rope will run over the gate, helped by the rope weight, its flicking action and the outwards trajectory of the climber, and will simply unclip itself.

In the following photographic sequence the leader has clipped the extender so that the rope runs along the back bar of the karabiner, but it has been clipped through from the front, not the back. Upwards movement of the climber could cause the extender to lift and rotate over the bolt, allowing the gate to be prised open. This could, in turn, cause the extender to completely unclip under its own weight, or if loaded by a falling climber.

An extender back-clipped, with the rope running behind the gate

(Top left) **Incorrect clipping. This can cause the extender to lift, rotating the karabiner clipped to the bolt.**

(Top right) **As the extender rotates, certain movements may cause it to lift up and across**

(Bottom left) **The extender ends up supported by its gate over the bolt hanger**

(Bottom right) **Downwards movement on the rope, such as a fall, can cause the karabiner to unclip from the bolt**

The third set of photographs shows, once again, an extender having been clipped away from the gate but through from the front to the back. Here, the lifting effect causes the karabiner connecting the extender to the bolt to rotate. Any change in direction of the run of the rope, caused by the climber moving across the route slightly or, more commonly, by the weight of the rope swinging across as the leader ascends, could then cause the extender tape to undo from the bolt karabiner.

(Top left) **The bolt is incorrectly clipped**

(Top right) **The tape of the extender can slip across the gate of the karabiner on the bolt**

(Bottom left) **The movement of the rope may let the tape of the extender cross the gate of the bolt karabiner**

(Bottom right) **Any sideways movement of the rope, or a fall, could cause the extender to unclip**

Pulling up the rope

If clipping into an extender has to be done from any distance below, as it will most likely have to be, you need to be able to efficiently pull through sufficient rope to enable this to happen. Having a belayer who is alert is essential, as there is nothing worse than pulling through an armful of rope only for it to stop halfway towards the extender as your belayer has dozed off in the sun. Almost as bad is the poor belaying technique where the rope is being paid out to you in 6in spurts,

Note

Take care to monitor the state of the inside radius of the karabiners that you use for clipping the bolts. Some hangers are quite sharp and can damage a karabiner in the event of a fall, causing the inside to burr. If this karabiner is subsequently used at the rope end of an extender the rope could become damaged. Similarly, if it were to be used at the placement end on a traditional route, such as being clipped into a wire, it could cause damage. Karabiners used on bolts should be kept for that purpose only and marked in some manner, perhaps with coloured tape. Alternatively, have a set of extenders used purely for bolt clipping and not for any other purpose.

making you hold on for what seems like forever as your belayer pulls through short sections at a time, possibly inhibited by a thick rope, inappropriate belay device or inexperience. A yell in the direction of your belayer will solve the first, better kit and experience will help to sort out the second.

However, there will be some instances where a single arm's length of rope will not suffice, as the extender to be clipped requires more than a single pull-through to reach it. Where only a small amount of rope is required over and above the normal pull-through – a few centimetres perhaps – it is possible to manipulate the rope through your hands, pulling it through with thumb and forefinger in order to get the right length. For situations where more rope is required, it is common to pull up a length, hold it in your teeth for a brief moment and reach down to pull up more. This works very well, and allows a good length of rope to be pulled through very quickly. It is extremely unlikely that more than one extra pull-through of rope is required..

If on a reasonable ledge when pulling through rope, it is fine to use the other hand – the one most likely holding onto the rock – to help. Here, trapping a bight of rope under the thumb whilst pulling through the next length of rope works well, but take care that you do not loosen your grip.

If you need to pull through some rope to make a clip, and find that you have not pulled through enough and thus elect to climb a little higher in order to reach, do not keep the rope in your hand as you move up. A fall here would result in a long drop with lots of slack in the system. Instead, drop the rope before moving and let your belayer take in any slack. You can then move up as normal whilst being belayed and, when repositioned, reach down and pull through however much rope is required.

Double-clipping a bolt in a crucial area, to prevent the rope from becoming detached

Double-clipping

Sometimes you may come across a move that takes quite a bit of thought, protected by a crucial bolt which, should it become unclipped for some reason, would mean you are liable for a significant fall. The type of move would be, perhaps, over a bulge, where it is difficult to be elegant, and you may have to drag yourself over the bolt and extender to gain height. In this situation – and for greater piece of mind – it may be worth double-clipping the bolt. This simply means that you clip it with two extenders, each orientated to face opposite directions. Make sure that you follow the rules for clipping, with the rope coming up from behind them. The chance of the rope undoing itself whilst you wrestle with the move is extremely slight. In the case of a hanger where only one karabiner will fit at a time, you may decide to use a screwgate and fix the extenders to this. Having ones with a loosely sewn loop will help here.

Stepping through

This is often done without thinking, and can result in a head or back injury if a fall is taken. It occurs when the leader, climbing above a bolt, places a foot or leg between the rope and the rock and then falls. His leg is trapped above the bolt and extender, which causes him to flip upside down and fall in a completely uncontrolled manner.

It is very important to be aware of where your foot is being placed when climbing above a bolt. Ensure that, should you need to use footholds on opposite sides of the rope, you place your leg around the outside of it and don't step through. A leader may become very involved in the technical side of climbing and momentarily forget where he is placing his feet, but the belayer will often be in a position to spot any potential problems and to let the leader know in time.

(Left) Do not place your foot inside the rope above an extender – it can result in you being tipped upside down in the event of a fall

(Right) Placing your foot outside the rope ensures that any fall will be clean

Holding an extender to clip

It is worth considering how best to hold a karabiner to clip it. It obviously takes some time to undo an extender from your harness, place it in the bolt, locate the rope, pull it through and clip it in, and anything that can be done to speed up this process is good. Consider that, whilst you are doing all of this with one hand, the other is holding onto the rock and is very probably getting tired. Fumbling at this point is not an option, and neither is back-clipping the extender, the consequences of which were covered earlier.

- **Method 1** This is the commonest, and seems to come naturally to most climbers. I find this to be the fastest and most efficient to execute, and with practice you can be clipping the extender almost subconsciously whist looking ahead and planning the next move. The rope is grasped between the thumb and forefinger and brought up to the gate side of the kara-biner, making sure that you are clipping through from the back. Place your middle finger in the karabiner and hold it steady, whilst pressing the rope onto the gate with your thumb. This will have the effect of making it drop in easily with a little help from gravity.

- **Method 2** In this the rope runs under your thumb and across the palm of your hand. Bring your palm up to the gate side of the karabiner and, grasping it firmly, use your thumb to squeeze the rope in through the gate. This is a little trickier to use, and practising the technique in advance helpful.

6

LEADING

STEP 1 Holding the rope between thumb and forefinger, keep the karabiner steady with your middle finger

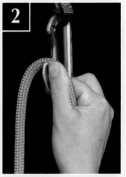

STEP 2 Using your thumb, press the rope onto the gate

METHOD 1

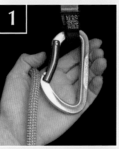

STEP 1 Hold the rope between your thumb and your palm

METHOD 2

STEP 2 Squeeze the karabiner and push the rope in with your thumb

STYLES OF ASCENT

On-sight

This is the smart name for simply turning up and leading the route from ground up, clipping the extenders into the bolts as you go and lowering off as normal, without any falls being taken. This is by far the commonest style of ascent, and what most people consider 'normal' climbing.

Bottom-roping

The technical side of setting up a bottom-rope system is covered in Chapter 5. It is often difficult to arrange to bottom-rope a climb in its entirety, unless someone has led the route in the first place and left the rope *in situ* through the lower-off point. This is because many sport climbs make the most of the best areas of rock, and may finish some distance below the top of a cliff or crag, with the ground between the lower-off and cliff top being loose, vegetated or otherwise undesirable to climb on. In some places it may be possible to reach down and clip the lower-off from the cliff top, but great care should be taken. Have a safety rope in place, safeguarding you against a slip whilst clipping the rope in.

Redpointing

The redpoint style of climbing is most often reserved for routes that are high up the grade scale. It denotes an ascent where the climb has been practised a number of times before the leader climbs the whole route in one go. Extenders may also have been pre-placed and simply clipped into whilst on the lead. The practice session/s may be on a bottom rope, or by the climber leading a short section, falling off and resting, then starting to climb again from the highpoint, linking up and memorising moves as he goes.

Using a clip stick

A clip stick is often employed in this style of climbing, as follows:

1   The first bolt will be clipped from the ground using the stick, with the rope already running through the extender.
2   The climber will then, with the help of the belayer, make his way up to the bolt, most likely by pulling on the rope and hoisting himself up.
3   Once there he clips himself into the same bolt with a cow's-tail. He then uses the clip stick to reach up and clip the second bolt, again with the rope in place.
4   Having undone the cow's-tail, he makes his way up to the second bolt and clips himself to it. This process is repeated until he reaches the lower-off.
5   Here he arranges the rope in the usual manner, either through the single point (if that is how the anchor is rigged) or by arranging his own gear so that the route can be bottom-roped without any chance of damaging the rope, as might happen with two independent staples.
6   He is lowered to the ground.

The climber can then practise the moves safely on a bottom rope, able to fall off, rest and repeat moves as required.

STEP 1 Starting to work on a route prior to a redpoint ascent

STEP 2 The climber pre-clips the bolts using a clip stick

STEP 3 He then 'works' the route, practising the moves with the security of a bottom rope

STEP 4 Finally, the route is led. Reaching the top will mean that the climb was successfully 'redpointed'.

When the climber is happy that he has all the moves 'taped' – he has worked out the sequences, how one move flows into another, where a rest is possible and the optimum position for clipping the extenders – he then leads the route. When he reaches the top, he makes any adjustments necessary to the lower-off and descends, stripping out the extenders on the way.

DEALING WITH BOLT PROBLEMS

Missing hangers

On some crags the first bolt hanger may be missing from routes. They may have been stolen, removed due to some access issues, or deliberately left off to deter people who are not climbers from 'having a go' and hurting themselves. On some routes hangers may have been left off for financial reasons, as fully equipping a long multi-pitch route is not cheap. Usually, if this situation is known, it will be highlighted in the guidebook.

A wire over a bolt stub. This should only be used in an emergency, and an alternative runner should be found quickly.

Carrying a spare hanger or two, as well as couple of 10 and 12mm nuts, may be prudent in some areas and on some routes, although most climbers would choose to ignore problem lines and climb elsewhere. If you are heading for a multi-pitch route and are expecting to have to place hangers, remember to have some means of tightening the nuts as you lead, as well as having your second being able to remove them again as he climbs past. You could always leave them in place if appropriate, and this will no doubt be appreciated by the person equipping the crag.

You can get round the problem of an unexpected missing hanger if you have a rack of wires. Push the head of a wire down a little to expose a loop. This can be fitted over the protruding bolt stub and the head then pushed back up to keep it in place. This is only a temporary measure and will never be as strong as a proper hanger, but it will do in an emergency. Find another anchor as soon as possible, maybe by placing a wire in a suitable crack, to minimise the chance of the wired bolt stub having to hold a fall. Be careful that the rope does not swing out too far from the cliff, as this could cause the wire to slip off.

Tip

A clip stick could be used to bypass the missing first bolt hanger, giving security from the second bolt for the initial section of the route.

Damaged hangers

You may come across a hanger that has been damaged. It could have been hit by rock fall and flattened, or perhaps – if a low-down bolt – vandalised. Often, the hanger will be bent to such an extent that it is impossible to clip a karabiner through it. To get over this problem, it would be handy to have a wire to hand. If the gap between the hanger and the rock is wide enough, push the wire down through the hole so that the head sits on top. The bottom section can now be clipped with a karabiner or extender as normal. If it has been badly damaged, push the head of the wire down slightly to expose a loop. Fit this upwards through the hole and clip a karabiner into it so that it cannot pull through. The bottom can now be clipped as before.

Note

If a hanger has been damaged in some way always be suspicious about the solidity of the rest of the placement. Expansion bolts in particular are prone to working loose, and if they have received a shock by being hit in a certain direction the strength of the entire placement could be compromised. If in any doubt, use another method of protection such as gear placed in a crack, or lower off and do another route. Don't assume that all such damaged placements are sound, even if they look as though they are.

BELAYING THE LEADER

Hard limestone climbing

7 BELAYING THE LEADER

The belayer has many responsibilities – it's not just a question of holding the rope for the leader. A belayer has a much harder job than the climber, as a good belayer will:

- Manage the rope effectively
- Pay out and take in the rope efficiently as required
- Watch out for any potential problems
- Be ready to hold a fall
- Control the leader as he is lowered off.

All of this with a bent neck, staring skywards and perhaps standing in the shade at the base of the crag, at the mercy of biting insects and annoyingly inquisitive dogs!

It is no wonder that many of the problems that occur with sport routes develop from issues concerning the belayer. To be able to belay effectively is no mean feat, and it takes a while to get to know the tricks of the trade and carry out your responsibilities safely and effectively. The following topics will highlight some of the skills needed, although experience is really the only way in which you can become proficient. One of the most important issues is trust. If you and your climbing partner trust each other to belay properly it does wonders for morale and confidence, and subsequently performance on the rock.

Using a rope mat and ground anchor, with a good braced posture

EFFECTIVE ROPE MANAGEMENT
This is the key to everything running efficiently. Simply dumping the rope on the ground and having the leader tie on is asking for trouble. The rope should be run through hand over hand into a neat pile at a point next to the belayer, with the leader tying onto the rope coming from the top of the pile. Alternatively – and a better system for single-pitch sport routes – is to have the rope in a rope bag which opens out into a flat sheet, keeping the rope clean whilst at the same time avoiding tangles.

GROUND ANCHORS

The mechanics of setting up ground anchors is covered in Chapter 4. However, it is worth mentioning again that a ground anchor may or may not be desirable, subject to a number of factors. If the leader is heavier than the belayer, or if the ground at the base of the climb is uneven or dangerous, it would be sensible to rig up a ground anchor. If, however, there is little chance of the belayer stumbling at the foot of the route and the leader is lighter, you may decide to do away with a ground anchor altogether. Do not take this decision lightly, as there is no doubt that a well-rigged ground anchor does much towards keeping the leader safe by keeping the second in place. However, a braced position and sound concentration can go a long way to making ground anchors unnecessary. Only you and your partner can decide, so consider the options and the possible outcome of your chosen course of action.

(Top left) **Good position when belaying from a ground anchor**

(Top right) **Non-dynamic position when belaying from a ground anchor in front**

(Bottom left) **Poor position, with the projecting rock at shin height posing a problem in the event of a fall**

(Bottom right) **Poor and inattentive belaying position, possibly resulting in injury to both party members**

SPOTTING

This is an important skill that is often overlooked as it does not involve any technical paraphernalia. Spotting is the safeguarding of a leader as he leaves the ground, prior to clipping the first bolt. For instance, if the first bolt is 3m above the ground, there is a chance that, should the leader slip, he could twist an ankle or worse, depending upon the landing site.

As the belayer is redundant until the first bolt is clipped, she can step in to help prevent any injury from occurring. She should take up position just behind the climber, arms outstretched and feet braced, one leg placed out behind, to give a solid base from which to field any slip. The purpose of spotting is not to catch the falling climber, as this would be physically impossible in most situations, but to a) guide him down onto a safe landing area and b) to stop him falling over backwards and possibly injuring his head or spine. It takes a little thought and some practice to become an efficient spotter, but if you have done this for companions whilst bouldering, for instance, you will have a good idea what to expect. Take care not to place yourself where you could be hurt by your falling companion.

The rope from your belay device should be slack enough to allow you to spot the leader without either of you getting tripped up, but short enough so that when he does clip the first bolt you can pull the rope through very quickly and start belaying as normal.

Spotting prior to clipping the first bolt. This is where the leader is at his most vulnerable, but the belayer should also watch out for his own security.

PAYING OUT THE ROPE

This is a pivotal area of belaying, and can be harder than at first imagined. Allowing the leader to ascend with enough rope so that he can move freely, but not so much that he is in danger of taking a long fall in the event of a slip, takes constant observation and adjustment. Also, being able to effectively manage the rope when the leader needs slack for a clip involves fine judgement, and the ability to pay out and take in rope through a belay device swiftly and safely.

If you are used to a standard belay device, perhaps as a traditional rock climber, you will find that there is little difference in that style of belaying and the style needed for clipping bolts. However, if you have decided to use an active belay device, the methods for paying out can vary (although taking in remains essentially the same as with a passive one).

Holding a Grigri in paying-out mode

Grigri device

The Grigri is an extremely popular active belay device, and many other styles have been modelled on it. Its advantage is that it has been designed to automatically lock off when loaded, allowing a belayer to hold the weight of a fallen or resting climber with ease. However, this locking-off mechanism can work against you: should the rope be pulled upwards from the device – as when a leader pulls through some slack to make a clip – it can lock off and he will be left in a precarious position with insufficient rope to clip in. Being alert as a belayer is going to help avoid this, and pre-empting when your leader is going to pull up the rope allows you to hold the device in a manner that prevents it from locking up.

Holding a Grigri in an alternative paying-out mode

The Grigri is not a hands-off device, so you cannot afford to let go of the dead rope (the one coming out of the back of the device to the rope pile). The best way to manage this is to hold the Grigri between thumb and forefinger, with your thumb holding down the lever arm to prevent it from lifting up into place. The dead rope is held below the device in your other three fingers, gripped very loosely. This allows you to pull the rope through with the other hand without it getting locked into place, giving slack to the leader as required. Once he has made the clip, you can take in any excess slack as usual.

SUM device

Another device style that is becoming popular is the SUM. This is extremely efficient at locking off, and works with ropes considerably thinner than those recommended for the Grigri. The difference is that the entire device has to be

7

BELAYING THE LEADER

Holding the SUM in the paying-out position

held in a certain position to allow the rope to run freely – not just the lever system, which only comes into play when locking off and lowering.

To safely pay out with the SUM, hold it between the thumb and forefinger, vertically out and downwards from your harness. The dead rope is again held between the three remaining fingers and allowed to run smoothly, but without losing control. The other hand now pulls up on the live rope (the one coming from the top of the device) and slack can be easily paid out. Should the leader slip at this point, the device will be pulled up out of your hand into the locked-off position, and only by pressing down on the lever or by the climber un-weighting the rope and you moving the device into a vertical position can the rope be moved again.

WATCHING FOR PROBLEMS

As a belayer you are in a good position to watch out for problems before, or as, they occur. These may include Z-clipping, back-clipping and stepping through the rope (see Chapter 6). A quick word from you will help to sort these out and prevent them from becoming real issues.

It may also be that you have a better view of the line of the route than the leader. Sometimes, if the climber is up close against the rock, a belayer has the ability to move around a little (unless attached to ground anchors), and be able to see the rest of the route more clearly than the climber. This becomes useful if the leader needs to know where the route goes (not always as obvious as it sounds), where the next bolt is or if he is missing an obvious handhold.

> **Tip**
>
> Clear and concise communication between belayer and climber is very important. Don't forget that the climber will be very involved in what he is doing, possibly some distance from you, and will not want to hold a protracted conversation just to get the basics of what needs to happen.

HOLDING A FALL

At some stage during your time as belayer you will have to hold your first leader fall. This may be a simple drop onto a bolt at the leader's waist level, or an impressive plummet from some height, perhaps occasioned by a slip whilst trying to clip a bolt high above. Whatever the cause the outcome should be the same: you successfully hold the fall, your companion feels a bit embarrassed, and either starts climbing again or is lowered to the ground.

It is very unusual for a climber to fall off without knowing it is about to happen. This is often preceded with a 'Watch me!' or similar, followed by a trip into the vertical. Even if a climber's foot slips from a hold, for example, he will often have a split second in which to call out and for you to react. If he is mentally in control of the climb but knows that he is going to drop off, a leader will normally shout 'Take!', indicating that he is on the way down.

Often, when climbing with traditional gear placements, a 'dynamic' belay is desirable. This means that the belayer allows a little slippage of the rope through the belay device in order to lessen the impact force on less-than-perfect running belays. In a sport-climb fall situation, the rope is often used as the main means of reducing the impact force, along with a lifting of the belayer as the rope becomes tight on her. It is often assumed that bolts are 100 percent safe – a very bold judgement to make – but generally the rope is simply held tight by the second and its elongation does the job of preventing the leader from injury. If an active belay device is being used, there is little choice but to let it lock off automatically, again relying on the rope to absorb the forces of the fall.

Your position as belayer is important, both for you and the leader. If you are holding the rope too slack or are some distance away from the foot of the route, the leader may fall quite a lot further than expected, especially if you are pulled off your feet and stumble forwards. There are ways of avoiding this:

- **Having a ground anchor** will help to prevent this, as will a stance near the base of the climb. Although being close in is not as crucial as with a traditionally protected route (where the further out you are the higher the chance of the protection being lifted up and out in the event of a fall), not being too far away is important. As the angle between you and the lowest clipped bolt increases, the more chance there is of you being pulled forwards, as opposed to upwards, and losing your footing. Many bolt types will have been placed in the rock at around 90 degrees, and so are very strong when pulled in that direction. If pulled outwards, however – as may occur in the event of a leader fall where the belayer is some way back from the cliff – there is a chance that previously weakened bolts could fail, in particular those relying on expansion friction to stay in place.

An extremely relaxed belaying manner – his partner was 10m up – not to be recommended!

- **If you do not have a ground anchor** in place, and your leader is telling you that he is about to fall off, make your way in close to the bottom of the route in preparation to take an upwards pull. Taking in the rope as you do so is obviously important, but do not be too eager to pull it all in tight. If the climber is above the last bolt you may pull him off, destroying the possibility that he could have regained his composure and stayed in contact with the rock after all.

Make sure that any loading on you, created by holding the fall, will not cause you to hurt yourself. Avoid standing directly underneath projections of rock, as the lift that you experience when holding the leader's weight may be sufficient for you to come into contact with it. A braced position, perhaps with one foot raised and placed against the wall in front of you, will offer the best stance.

Once the leader has fallen, give him a while to decide what he wants to do next. He may wish to come down for a rest, or perhaps want to get back on the rock and try the move again. It is worth encouraging him to hang on the rope for a few moments and shake out, relaxing and resting his arm muscles, before continuing on and up.

LOWERING THE LEADER

At some stage the leader is going to have to be lowered. He has completed the route and wants to lower off, perhaps he's got part way and given up, or maybe he is working a route which would therefore involve a certain amount of up and down. Whatever the reason, as belayer you will have a little more notice than if you were holding a leader fall. Again, having a ground anchor in place will help you to stay in balance, especially if the climber is heavier than you.

If you do not have a ground anchor (the norm in most cases) move close into the base of the climb. This means that you will be pulled upwards by the weight of the leader, not inwards. Bracing a foot forwards on the rock, in a similar fashion to that adopted when holding a fall, will help keep you stable.

If you are using a conventional passive belay device, lowering should not present any problems. Keep both hands on the dead rope and feed it through gently, avoiding the temptation to let it run too fast. You may need to stop at intervals to allow the climber to remove extenders as he reaches them.

Lowering with an active belay device

If you are using an active belay device, perhaps a Grigri or SUM, lowering is carried out in a slightly different manner. It is important that the cam-releasing handle of the Grigri is not used as the brake, but that you control the descent of the climber by holding the dead rope over the roll bar to the right of the body of the device. The cam is there as a

(Below left) **Using the Grigri to lower a climber. A braced body position is important for the belayer in order to remain stable.**

(Below right) **Lowering a climber using the SUM. The belayer being in a good braced position is, again, very important.**

lock-off brake if things get out of control. Problems could occur if the handle is being used to control the rate of descent, as there is little difference between 'slow' and 'full speed'. It is essential that you have practised with the Grigri before using it for real for the first time.

The SUM requires a slightly different action. To release the handle you need to push down on it from above, and this requires quite a bit of force if you are holding a heavy climber. It can, however, be used either left- or right-handed. The rate of descent can be controlled both by depressing the handle for the required distance as well as the rate with which you feed the dead rope into it.

Unclipping during descent

8 LOWERING OFF

(Opposite)
Lowering off from a steep route

It must be emphasised that the process of lowering off is one that should be undertaken with the utmost care and a high degree of checking and double-checking of systems. More accidents occur during lowering than during any other part of the sport-climbing session. Common errors include:

- Leader untying the rope and dropping it, leaving himself marooned.
- Leader attempting to rethread a lower-off without clipping himself in with a cow's-tail, and falling off at a critical point.
- Leader not retying back into the correct part of his harness, leading to failure when the system is loaded.
- Leader and belayer not communicating effectively.
- Leader having pushed onto a higher lower-off, which prevents him from being lowered to the ground with a single rope length.
- The end of the rope not being secured, either with a knot or to the belayer, with the end subsequently running through the belay device on a long lower.
- Inefficient lower-off point or poor threading method, meaning that the climbing rope jams, often at a chain link, leaving the leader marooned.

These can all be avoided through practice, discussion, attentive belaying and sensible route choice.

For the majority of sport routes lowering-off is unavoidable. In many cases it would be extremely dangerous, if not impossible, to attempt to climb on and out, as the terrain will most likely deteriorate and the consequences of a fall become dire.

There are a number of ways to prepare for lowering, depending on the style of lower-off point and the equipment provided. Some climbs will feature a system where the rope can be simply and quickly clipped into a snaplink of some description, or is placed over and around a captive stud, often with 'arms' to keep the rope in place during the lower. Other styles require the climber to untie from the climbing rope and thread it through one or two rings, retying on the other side before descending. Problems will most likely

occur with this latter method, although prior practice and careful checking whilst carrying out the procedure will help to negate any dangers.

PRE-CLIMB PREPARATION

The main preparation for the lower is the inclusion of a cow's-tail on the harness. This will be used to clip the leader into the lower-off point or nearby bolt whilst he arranges the rope for the descent.

- The simplest cow's-tail is a 120cm sling lark's-footed around the abseil loop on the harness. This sling is then equipped with a screwgate karabiner to provide security at the top anchor. The screwgate can be clipped onto a gear loop at the side of the climber's harness, underneath any extenders, ready for use. The thinner the sling the more likely it will get tangled in other equipment on the gear loops, so a wide tape is often preferred.

- Alternatively, a length of rope can be used to similar effect. One end is secured around the front of the harness, the other has a figure of eight knot tied in it and is equipped with a screwgate, clipping into a gear loop as before. The advantage of using the rope system is that almost any length can be used, cut and tied to a predetermined length. A 120cm sling is ideal if the clipping-in point is directly in front of the leader, but if a reach has to be made the flexibility of a longer cow's-tail will be appreciated.

- A third option is to use a longer sling that comes ready-sewn in a series of loops. This caters for a range of distances, albeit with a bit of fiddling to get the initial length correct. Care should be taken that the sling is clipped in the correct manner, not with the karabiner loading the stitched section in a dangerous way.

It is also important to have a good screwgate karabiner on the harness, kept out of the way round the back. This will be used to clip the rope to the climber when using the figure of eight rethreading method.

LOWER-OFF SET-UPS

Clip-in style lower-off

This style of top anchor is by far the easiest to clip and rarely presents the climber with any difficulty. In its simplest form it will consist of a single drilled bolt with an integral snapgated

Cow's-tail ready for use, lark's-footed to the harness

Clip-in style lower-off

steel karabiner, and the climber simply has to clip it in the normal manner and be lowered off. There are various designs of single-point clip lower-offs, but all work in a similar way. Often a chain will be used to bring two bolts down to one point, where the clip-in karabiner will be situated.

Slightly more complicated is the 'pig's-tail' ('calf's-tail') style lower-off. This typically consists of a bent metal bar, shaped to hold the rope at its lower curve, and a surrounding 'guard rail', designed to prevent the rope from flicking out of place. In addition, some designs also have metal 'shoulders' that prevent the rope from rolling up and over the top, making for a very secure point. Placing the rope around the pig's-tail may take a few seconds, and if the climber is not on a ledge or is otherwise insecure he should have a safeguard in place in case of a slip.

In some cases a bolt will have been placed next to the lower-off. This allows either an extender or, more securely, a cow's-tail, to be clipped in, providing security whilst the rope is arranged at the anchor.

Putting the rope into a tail-shaped lower-off

Rethread style lower-off

This requires some thought as to how to best approach the necessary rope management, along with the obvious concern for the safety of the climber. Clipping into the point with a cow's-tail – be it a chain or one or two individual bolts – will almost always be necessary, unless the anchor is above a large ledge where the climber can stand and work safely. Even here it would be sensible to clip in with a cow's-tail in case of a slip.

Bolt next to a lower-off, useful for clipping the cow's-tail into when rigging the lower

Two methods of organising the rope are given below, relevant for slightly different situations. These should be practised in a safe environment at low level to ensure that the routine is both safe and slick: a mistake at the top of a route can mean at best the loss of the rope, at worst a fall. These two methods assume that the lower-off is constructed from two bolts linked together with a chain, and a large ring placed between them through which the rope must be threaded to allow the lower to take place.

> ### Tip
> With all methods it is essential to double-check the system before committing bodyweight to it.

Figure of eight method

This is the commonest way to arrange the rope at the top of a route, and can be quite quick to organise.

1   The climber, having arrived at the top of the route, makes himself safe by clipping into the anchor with a cow's-tail. The length of this cow's-tail should allow him to reach the anchor easily when snug, but not be so loose as to make slipping and shock-loading the system

a possibility. At this point the climber can tell his belayer that he is connected to the anchor so that she can relax. She should not disconnect any part of the belay system until the entire lower is finished.

2   The climber passes a bight of the climbing rope through the ring on the chain and ties a figure of eight knot in it.

3   A screwgate karabiner is clipped through the figure of eight, which is in turn clipped onto the abseil loop on the climber's harness.

FIGURE OF EIGHT METHOD

1 Having clipped in with a cow's-tail, thread a bight of rope through the ring.

2 Tie a figure of eight on this bight.

3 Clip it into the abseil loop using a screwgate.

4 Untie from the end of the climbing rope.

5 Pull the end through the ring and tuck it into the harness to keep it out of the way.

6 Having tested the system, unclip the cow's-tail and descend.

4   The main knot connecting the climber's harness to the rope can now be untied. There will now be a tail of rope. This is pulled through the ring and is best tucked into a gear loop or the harness waistband to prevent any chance of it catching or the climber tripping over it during descent.

5   Communicating with the belayer, the climber moves up close to the chain so that any slack in the system can be taken in. Committing his weight to it, the climber checks that the rope is correctly arranged and that he is safe to be lowered. Should there be any question as to his security he is still connected by the cow's-tail, thus any adjustments can be safely made.

6   Once the climber is happy that the system will operate properly, he communicates once more with his belayer, removes the cow's-tail and can be lowered to the ground.

Tie-in method
There may be a situation where the climber opts to tie into the end of the rope rather than use a karabiner to connect himself. This may be because he needs the full rope length to make it back to the ground, or because the screwgate karabiner has been forgotten or used on another part of the climb.

1   Arriving at the top of the route, the climber secures himself to the chain with a cow's-tail, taking into consideration the points noted as for the figure of eight method above.

2   Using this method there is a chance of dropping the rope accidentally. In order to prevent this, a bight of rope from 1m or so down is pulled up and a figure of eight or overhand knot on the bight is tied in it. This is then clipped onto a suitable point such as the chain or a nearby bolt with an extender or screwgate. Thus, if the rope is dropped during the next procedure it won't be lost down the route.

3   Untying from the rope, the end is passed through the ring.

4   The climber now reattaches himself to the rope. This can be accomplished either by redoing the knot directly onto the harness, or by tying a figure of eight on the bight and clipping it into the abseil loop with a screwgate.

5   The back-up knot, connecting the rope to the anchor to prevent loss, can now be unclipped and untied, with the extender or screwgate being retrieved.

8

LOWERING OFF

TIE-IN METHOD

1 Having made yourself safe with a cow's-tail, clip the rope into an extender to avoid dropping it.

2 Untie from the rope and thread it through the ring.

3 Retie into the harness.

4 After removing the extender and testing the system, remove the cow's-tail and descend.

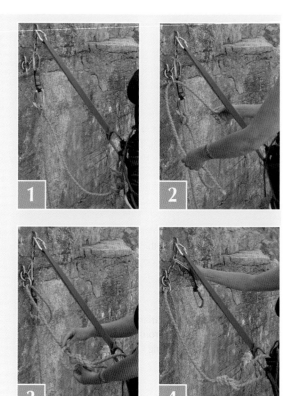

6   After communicating with his belayer the climber moves up close to the chain so that any slack in the system can be taken in. Committing his weight to it, the climber checks that the rope is correctly arranged and that he is safe to be lowered. Should there be any question as to his security, he is still connected by the cow's-tail, thus any adjustments can be safely made.

7   Once the climber is happy that the system will operate properly, he communicates once more with the belayer, removes the cow's-tail and can be lowered to the ground.

A slight variation on the above method is as follows:

•   Instead of clipping the rope into an extender to avoid losing it, pass a bight through the ring and tie a figure of eight in it.
•   Clip this to your abseil loop with a screwgate.
•   Untie from the rope, pull the end through and retie.

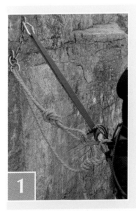

VARIATION

1 Thread a bight of rope through the ring and clip it to your harness.

2 Untie from the rope, pull it through the ring and retie.

- Undo the screwgate and the figure of eight.
- The slack rope is taken in by the belayer and, after all the appropriate checks are made, descent can go ahead as normal.

The main advantage of this variation is that the rope is continuously connected to a strongpoint on the harness, in case anything should go wrong with the cow's-tail.

Ring-bolt lower-off

The tops of some routes are equipped with two ring-bolts but no connecting chain or other linkage. This is often due to financial reasons, as equipping a number of routes with chains will prove quite expensive. If this is the case either of the above two methods can be used, depending upon whether the climber wishes to tie onto the end of the rope or clip in with a karabiner.

1 The cow's-tail is clipped into one of the bolts. Communication with the belayer should take place as outlined above.
2 In order to prevent the rope being dropped, a figure of eight or overhand knot is tied onto a bight of rope and an extender or screwgate clipped in. As the eye of the bolts through which the rope is later to be passed may be quite small (and to avoid clutter) the karabiner securing the rope can be clipped to the cow's-tail screwgate.
3 Untying from the rope, the end is passed through both of the rings. The climber now reattaches himself to the rope, either by redoing the knot directly onto the harness, or by tying a figure of eight on the bight and clipping it into the abseil loop with a screwgate.

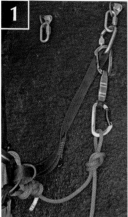 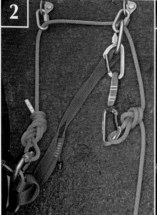 

1 Clip in with a cow's-tail and secure the climbing rope.

2 Untie from the rope, thread it through the anchors and retie or clip in with a screwgate.

3 Take off the extender and any knot, unclip the cow's-tail and descend.

4   The back-up knot, connecting the rope to the anchor to prevent loss, can now be unclipped and untied, with the extender or screwgate being retrieved.

5   After communicating with the belayer the climber moves up close to the bolts so that any slack in the system can be taken in.

6   Committing his weight to it, the climber checks that the rope is correctly arranged and that he is safe to be lowered. Should there be any question as to his security he is still connected by the cow's-tail, thus any adjustments can be safely made.

7   Once the climber is happy that the system will operate properly, he communicates once more with the belayer, removes the cow's-tail and can be lowered to the ground.

Bottom roping

It may be that the climbing team wishes to use the rope as a bottom rope, where it will be left in place for other climbers to use without them having to resort to leading. If so the extenders placed on the original lead are best removed as the first climber is lowered off. Care should be taken when removing the lowest of the extenders, as there will most likely be a tight angle where the rope runs through it and up the route. If possible, the belayer should move close into the base of the climb to allow the leader to remove the bottom extender easily, avoiding the bow-string-like whip of the rope in the process.

If the route is overhanging for any distance it may be difficult for the person being lowered to reach the extenders to unclip them. To solve this, he can clip a spare extender between his abseil loop and the rope so that it runs freely. As he descends, his weight on the climbing rope keeps it tight and the extender keeps him close to the rock.

Steep routes

On steep routes where the first bolt is near the ground, there is a chance that the climber being lowered could swing out once he has unclipped it and hit the ground due to the arc and rope stretch. Either of the following could remedy the problem:

Using an extender to pull in close to bolts when being lowered

8

LOWERING OFF

- Leave it in place if it is only a short distance up on easy terrain, be lowered to the ground, then climb up again to unclip it from below.
- Leave the second or third in place with the rope in, descend to the first extender and remove it, go back up to the one left in and unclip from there. This means that any swing will be much higher up, with far less chance of hitting anything under rope stretch.

If stripping out extenders in order to bottom-rope a steep route, consideration should be given to the possibility of the subsequent climber swinging out from the route and injuring himself on a section of rock or other obstruction, such as a tree. In this case, one or two key extenders can be left in position to keep the rope in place. Once the climber has finished the route, he will be able to swing back in whilst being lowered and either remove the extenders or reclip them for a subsequent ascent.

Note

You may see people using two extenders clipped together being used as a cow's-tail. Very often one end will be in the anchor, the two bentgate karabiners will be clipped into each other and the other karabiner clipped into their harness. This is a very dangerous way to 'protect' yourself, as whilst you move about near the anchor the karabiners could cross over each other and undo, leaving you totally vulnerable to a fall.

LOWERING OFF FROM AN INTERMEDIATE BOLT

Using a bolt as the anchor for a lower may become necessary when retreating from a route. Perhaps the route is too difficult for the leader, he is off route, or there are weather or daylight considerations.

Lowering from a single bolt will never be as satisfactory as using a purpose-designed station. However, this does happen so it is best to be prepared. If the leader is to be lowered with the intent that the belayer will then take over and complete the route, nothing more needs to be done. The bolt is clipped with an extender in the usual manner and the climber can descend. If this is not the case, and none of the climbing team is going to carry on up the route, a slightly different approach is needed.

It should be noted that all of the following could be avoided if the leader was able to reverse, or down-climb, the ground he had just covered. Having decided to bail out he climbs to below the top extender, reaches up and unclips it from the bolt. At the same time, the belayer takes in all the slack, taking care not to pull the leader off. The leader now climbs down to below the next bolt and the process is repeated. If this is not possible, as the climbing would be too hard, a technical solution needs to be found. The ease with which the leader can organise the lower depends very much on the size of eye in the bolt to which the rope is to be attached.

Bent hangers

With a normal bent metal hanger there may be room for only one karabiner. The team will probably not wish to abandon an expensive quick-draw, so this can be substituted for by an old karabiner or a maillon, carried at the back of the harness for this purpose. Up to this point it may have been used to attach the chalk bag to the climber's harness, for instance, and can therefore be sacrificed. With this type of bolt hanger, it is essential that a karabiner or maillon is used and the rope is not simply threaded through the eye. The narrow radius and sharp edges common to this type could easily cut through the rope if it were loaded, and the rope sheath would almost certainly be severed during a weighted lower. Quite apart from this, retrieving the rope when the leader reached the ground may well prove impossible due to friction.

Initial clipping

The leader may well have decided prior to arriving at the bolt that he is going to descend, and in this case he would simply clip straight in with the old karabiner and go down. If he made the decision after clipping the bolt with an extender, this would have to be changed prior to the descent, or abandoned. The clipping point for some bolts may often allow the use of good holds, so the swap from extender to karabiner can be made. However, the safety of the leader is paramount so no desperate gymnastics should be attempted if there is any chance of him falling a distance whilst unclipped from the bolt. Abandoning the extender, or perhaps retrieving it later by abseil, would be the safest plan. It may be possible to clip the upper karabiner (the one that goes into the hanger) and retrieve the rest of the extender and lower karabiner by sliding it off. Watch out for your own safety if doing this.

Clipping large-eye bolts

If the eye of the bolt allows for two karabiners to be clipped in, the leader can operate in a safer manner. Once the decision has been made to go down, he can clip his cow's-tail into the bolt eye. This should be done underneath the extender already clipped in, as this will need to be removed in due course. Once the extender has been taken away, the old spare screwgate is put into position and the rope clipped into this.

1   The climber clips his cow's-tail into the eye of the bolt. This should be positioned underneath the extender already there, otherwise the latter will be difficult to take out.
2   The rope is unclipped from the extender that is removed from the bolt.
3   The spare karabiner is clipped into the bolt. If possible, this should be positioned underneath the cow's-tail karabiner. Care should be taken that only a downwards loading is maintained on the bolt.

The rope should never be threaded directly through the eye of a thin bolt hanger

A karabiner or maillon should be used to prevent the rope from being cut

LOWERING FROM A LARGE-EYE BOLT

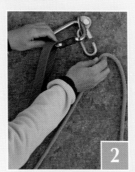

2 Remove the extender and put a spare karabiner or maillon in its place.

1 Clip the cow's-tail into the bolt underneath the extender.

3 Having clipped the rope in, take off the cow's-tail and descend.

4   The climbing rope is placed into the karabiner.

5   The climber pulls himself towards the bolt sufficiently so that the belayer can take in the rope tight, freeing the cow's-tail.

6   This is then unclipped and the climber can be lowered.

Threading the rope through a bolt

If the bolt has a smooth and wide inner surface, such as with an 8 or 10mm ring-bolt, the rope may, in some cases, be placed directly through this. It is essential that the inner surface is smooth and rounded, otherwise the rope could become damaged or cut during the lower. Metal bolt heads that are smooth but of less than 8mm diameter may be too thin given the loading they have to take, and will consequently damage the rope.

1   The climber clips his cow's-tail into the eye of the bolt. This should be positioned underneath the extender already there, otherwise the latter will be difficult to take out.

2   The rope is unclipped from the extender that is removed from the bolt.

3   A bight of rope is tied into an overhand or figure of eight knot and clipped onto an extender, which is in turn clipped onto a suitable point near the anchor. This

THREADING THROUGH A BOLT

1 Having clipped in the cow's-tail, secure the climbing rope with an extender.

2 Untie from the climbing rope, thread it through the bolt and retie.

3 Remove the extender and any extra knots, remove the cow's-tail and descend.

may best be positioned on the screwgate karabiner on the cow's-tail. This ensures that the rope is not dropped.

4 The climber unties from the rope and threads the end through the bolt, either retying on the other side or clipping into his abseil loop with a figure of eight on the bight connected with a screwgate karabiner.

5 The knot safeguarding the rope and its accompanying extender can be removed.

6 Pulling himself into the bolt, ensuring a downwards pull at all times, the climber removes the cow's-tail.

7 He can now be lowered.

Note

The utmost care should be taken to ensure the rope is not lost during this procedure, hence clipping it to the cow's-tail with an extender. If the rope is dropped the leader will be left marooned and in a dire situation.

Considerations

It should be emphasised that a single bolt on a route is not the ideal point from which to lower off, and that the methods above should only be employed if there is no alternative. Great care should be taken to ensure that any loading on the bolt, created by the climber whilst arranging the rope, is in a downwards direction. It may not have been placed to take an outward pull, unlike those at top anchors which often have the bolts drilled on a suitable piece of rock at an almost vertical angle.

Think about the stability of the bolt from which the climber is being lowered. Normally, the lower extenders would be stripped out as the climber descends. However, if the top bolt were of questionable strength removing the lower runners would not be a good idea. If the first runner down is removed and the top bolt fails, the climber will end up falling a considerable distance. This distance will dramatically increase with every extender subsequently stripped out, and a ground fall will very quickly become a possibility. To prevent this some options are available, although none is particularly satisfactory.

Stripping the route from below
If the bolts only have a small hole in the hanger, admitting only one karabiner at a time, the best option is as follows. This assumes that the ground immediately surrounding the leader is irreversible and far harder than the rest of the route.

1   The climber is lowered to the ground.
2   He unties from the rope that is then pulled through.
3   The climber reties and climbs the lower part of the route, clipping the existing extenders that are still in place, all but the top one.
4   When he reaches the final hanging extender, he unclips this whilst protected from below.
5   He now down-climbs, unclipping as he passes extenders, and repeats the process as required.

This procedure relies on a number of factors, not least that the climber is happy enough to reach up and unclip an extender above him. The nature of the ground also needs to be sufficiently forgiving for this to be carried out, once the terrain around the top bolt has been bypassed by being lowered. If this is not the case, the options are to retrieve equipment by abseil or, if this is not practical, to abandon the gear. One possible further option is to use a clip stick that has the facility for unclipping karabiners from bolts, although this may be impractical for a number of reasons (such as sourcing one in the first place).

Reversing bolt by bolt
If the bolts are of a size to hold both karabiner and rope, such as with the smooth ring-bolts, a more secure method can be used. This will assume that the option of down-climbing and removing the extenders from below is not practical.

1   The climber arranges the rope through the ring-bolt as outlined above.

2   He descends to the next bolt and clips in with the cow's-tail before removing the extender.

3   Pulling up a bight of rope, he ties an overhand or figure of eight knot in it and clips it to an extender, which is in turn clipped to a suitable point, most likely the cow's-tail karabiner. This is to ensure that the rope is not lost.

4   The climber unties from the rope and pulls it through from the bolt above.

5   He threads the end of the rope through the bolt next to him and either reties or clips into his abseil loop with a figure of eight on the bight and a screwgate karabiner.

6   Pulling up towards the bolt, ensuring a downwards loading, he unclips the cow's-tail.

7   Depending on the situation, he can now be lowered all the way, stripping out the extenders as he goes. Alternatively, if the properties of the bolt through which his rope is threaded is still questionable, he repeats the process for the next bolt down and so on, until safety is reached.

This procedure is far from satisfactory and extremely time-consuming, but may be the only option if all other alternatives have been considered and found to be inappropriate.

Note

One method for retreating from narrow or sharp-edged hangers uses a sling threaded through in a manner that means it can be abseiled on and then pulled through and retrieved. This is *not* recommended for the following reasons:

• The loading on the sling – particularly a thin Dyneema type (suggested by some as being the best for this technique) – could easily be sufficient to cut right through it under bodyweight on the hanger edges.

• The uneven loading of the action of abseiling will increase this possibility.

You can only descend a third of the rope length, as opposed to half if being lowered.

• A sling used in this manner will probably have to be discarded when retrieved due to damage to the fibres, which will cost you over twice as much as abandoning a karabiner or maillon.

Always err on the safe side and don't ever trust loaded slings over sharp edges.

8

LOWERING OFF

Note

Although lowering from a single point might seem like the best option, if there is any question as to the security of either the system or the bolt, down-climbing would definitely be better. This would not only prevent loading the bolt but would also help to avoid any damage to the rope. The possible abandonment of gear is better than risking your own life to save a bit of money.

LOWERING FROM STANCES ON A MULTI-PITCH ROUTE

Although abseiling will often be the preferred method of descent, lowering one or more climbers from a series of intermediate stances whilst descending a multi-pitch route may be the option for some parties. The lowering may be carried out in a semi-direct belay manner (with the load being taken by a belay device on the belayer's harness) but a direct belay is far more efficient, with the weight of the person being lowered going straight to the anchor. The vast majority of intermediate stances will be equipped with a substantial anchor point, very often two bolts linked with a chain and ring. It is assumed that this style of anchor is used for all the following procedures.

The advantages of the direct belay system are:

• The entire load is taken by the anchor, giving the belayer a more comfortable time.
• The belayer is free to move around within the constraints of the stance, enabling her to organise the lower easily from a variety of positions.

There are several ways in which the rope can be organised at the stance:

• **Italian hitch lower** This uses minimal equipment, although there is a tendency for the rope to twist over long distances. Careful rope management and untwisting at each stance is important.

• **Belay device lower** This is smooth and efficient and does not twist the rope.

• **Self-locking active belay device lower** Devices such as the Grigri and the SUM fall into this category. They give a good, controlled lower, but with a weight penalty.

Those embarking on long technical multi-pitch routes are more likely to have the lighter belay device with them.

For the purposes of the following it is assumed that a two-person team is on a route that offers a good anchor, two bolts brought down to a ring via a chain, on reasonable ledges.

Italian hitch lower
An HMS screwgate karabiner should be used, and this will be clipped into an appropriate part of the anchor. The person controlling the lower should ensure his own security, probably by clipping a cow's-tail into the anchor as well.

- The wide end of the HMS needs to be positioned away from the anchor, so that the Italian hitch will run smoothly when the system is loaded. It is useful, for ease of clipping, if the gate opens towards the bottom.
- The rope should be run through to ensure there are no kinks or knots, and arranged so that the person being lowered is connected to the end of rope coming out from the top of the pile. The rope should be sorted in an area appropriate to the size of the stance, not under the climber's feet but also not out of reach.
- As maximum friction with an Italian hitch is with the controlling (dead) rope parallel with the one holding the person descending (live rope), the belayer should position herself on the downhill side of the anchor system.
- The person being lowered can be tied into his harness in a normal fashion, or can be attached via a figure of eight knot and a screwgate karabiner clipped to the abseil loop on his harness.
- Once the Italian hitch is connected to the HMS and the person to be lowered is tied or clipped on, he can descend. The best method for controlling the rope is to have both hands on the dead rope and slowly feed it out.

Lowering off using an Italian hitch

Belay device lower
The set-up at the stance can be similar to that outlined for the Italian hitch lower. However, the person controlling the descent must be able to provide efficient braking by bringing the dead rope running out from the device back at an angle of 180°, opposite to that of the Italian hitch. If there is sufficient room on the stance it may be possible just to arrange the belay device a little closer to the edge, giving the belayer space in which to manoeuvre the dead rope. If space is limited, or for some other reason the belay device

Tip
When using the Italian hitch lower the rope may become twisted over time. Allow the rope to untwist at each stance before commencing the next part of the descent.

Lowering off using a belay device with the dead rope clipped back to a karabiner through the chain from the anchor

Tip

Whenever both climbers are at a stance and pulling the rope through, make sure that there is no chance of dropping it down the crag and becoming stranded. Clip the rope to a suitable part of the anchor before starting to pull it down.

must be set tight back against the back wall of the ledge, a slightly different system can be set up.

- The belay device is clipped to the ring on the chain and the rope placed through in the usual manner.
- A second karabiner is attached to one of the ring-bolts, and the rope clipped in.
- The belayer can then position herself in front of the belay device, as the dead rope (controlling descent) runs from her, through the ring-bolt karabiner, and into the belay device. The dead rope is automatically set in the braking position and the weight of the person descending can be easily held.

If it is not possible to clip a karabiner through the chain for some reason, a similar result can be attained by using a sling.

- The sling is clipped into the ring on the chain, with the device being placed on the other end of the sling. This need not be any great length – around 30cm will suffice.
- A second screwgate karabiner is clipped into the ring.
- The rope from the person being lowered is run through the belay device as normal, and the dead rope is taken back and through the karabiner on the ring.
- The belayer can then operate from a position in front of the device, as the dead rope will be running via the screwgate in the correct manner for braking.

Some karabiners have been designed with a captive section through which the rope can run. This allows the same braking effect mentioned above to be achieved, without having to clip in extra karabiners to the system or use a sling.

(Left) Lowering off using a belay device and a karabiner clipped into a sling for control

(Right) Lowering off using a Frieno karabiner

Note

If lowering a novice down to an intermediate stance, make sure he knows how to make himself safe, most likely by clipping in with a cow's-tail. A short briefing and dry run at the original stance will help ensure his safety and avoid possible misunderstanding.

Self-locking active belay device lower

These devices are useful for lowering, but remember that their auto-locking properties do not allow for a hands-off approach. For instance, once the person to be lowered is clipped into the system, the belayer should not release her hold on the dead rope for any reason, even though the device may appear to auto-lock efficiently on its own.

Lowering using an active self-locking belay device (SUM)

- The device is clipped into the anchor. It should be remembered that the belayer must be able to reach the device for the lower to take place, so adjusting its position with the use of a sling may be appropriate in some circumstances.
- Most devices of this type rely on a mechanical distortion of part of the body to provide the braking effect. Great care should be taken to ensure that the device is well away from any sections of rock that could hamper this movement, render it useless and make the rope impossible to hold.
- Holding the dead rope in the appropriate manner, depending upon the type of device being used, gently commence the lower. This will probably mean that the belayer is holding the weight of the person descending, with the device being used as a 'dead-man's handle' (a failsafe back-up) in case of a problem occurring.

Lowering off using a Grigri

The person operating the lower could be lowered by the person now below him, if appropriate. This may save the trouble of having to organise an abseil rig.

1   Once the person being lowered has reached the next stance, the belayer ties an overhand knot in the dead rope and clips it into a suitable point on the anchor. This will avoid the rope being dropped down the crag.
2   The belayer disassembles the lowering system, removing all equipment.
3   The end of the rope is threaded through the ring on the anchor chain, and she ties or clips herself to it.

Tip

Those of a nervous disposition find lowering very worrying. Allow them to have all their weight on the system before starting to pay the rope out slowly and steadily. They may find it difficult to maintain their footing if the rope is paid out too fast.

8

LOWERING OFF

4 The climber on the stance below takes in all the rope between the two of them and, after appropriate communication, the person above can be lowered.

5 Once they are down and safe, the rope can be untied and pulled through.

Note

Once the person has been lowered, it is likely that the belayer will have to abseil in order to join him. It is important to think about this when selecting an intermediate ledge on the descent. If the rope is 60m long and a suitable ledge 50m down, and the leader were to abseil on a doubled rope, he will only descend for 30m, ending up some distance above his companion. However, on rigged abseil stations it may be appropriate to lower the first person past the first point to the next. This will save time as the belayer can then join his colleague in two abseils for the one lower.

Note

In a multi-pitch situation make sure that the rope reaches a safe stance at an appropriate point. This may best be measured by dropping the tail of the rope down as a gauge before rigging the system, with care being taken to ensure that there is no chance of the rope getting stuck when it is pulled back up.

LOWERING TWO PEOPLE AT ONCE

It may sometimes be necessary for two people to be lowered at the same time, thus speeding up the overall descent time. This could be due to a number of factors, for instance fading daylight. This technique should not be used until it has been practised in a safe situation, as the control and concentration needed by the belayer is far greater than when dealing with one person. This is often considered to be the preserve of a qualified and experienced instructor. It works best on simple slab routes, where the people being lowered can keep their footing all the way and so make the process easier.

The lowering section of the system can be set up as detailed above, using either an Italian hitch, belay device or self-locking active belay device. The difference will be the attachment of the two people to the end of the rope, and two systems are suitable.

Using rope

- Approximately 3m of rope is doubled back on itself, and tied off halfway along its length with an overhand knot to give a 1.5m loop with a 1.5m tail (see photograph below).
- One of the people being lowered is clipped into the loop with a screwgate karabiner attached to his harness.
- The other person is attached to the tail of the rope, either by tying a figure of eight on the bight into it and clipping in with a screwgate, or by tying directly into the harness in a conventional manner.
- The overhand knot can be adjusted as required, giving some leeway as to the positioning of the two people. It may be found that having one a short distance above the other is the most efficient.

Using a 240cm sling

- A figure of eight on the bight is tied on the end of the rope.
- An overhand or figure of eight knot is tied onto the midway point of the sling.
- This is then clipped onto the end of the rope, using a screwgate karabiner.
- The two people descending clip onto either side of the sling with screwgate karabiners.

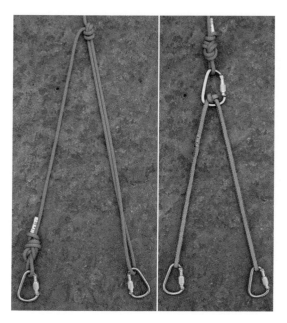

(*Left*) **Using the rope to connect two people when lowering**

(*Right*) **Using a sling with overhand knot to connect two people to the rope when lowering**

8

LOWERING OFF

Tip

If the rope is to be pulled up once the first person has descended, ensure that he has untied all of the knots in it. If not the rope could jam and become irretrievable.

Note

It is essential that the end of the rope on the controlling side be secured so that it cannot run through the belay device should control be lost. The belayer could be tied to the end in the conventional manner or, more likely, the rope be clipped into an appropriate part of the anchor with a karabiner and overhand or figure of eight knot.

9 MULTI-PITCH ROUTES

At some stage during your sport-climbing career you will probably want to try your hand at multi-pitch routes. A multi-pitch route is anything that is more than one rope length in height, therefore requiring one or more intermediate stances. Such a route may have only two pitches, or twenty or more. The climbing process would normally follow one of the two systems:

Leading through (swinging leads)
1   The leader climbs the first pitch and belays on a prepared stance.
2   The second comes up to join him.
3   They swap leads, where the second now becomes the leader and collects the gear before setting off on the next pitch.
4   At the next stance she belays, the second comes up, collects the gear and leads on and up the next pitch.
5   This continues until both reach the top of the climb.
6   They descend, either by walking off or by abseil.

Leading on
1   The leader climbs the first pitch and belays.
2   The second climbs up.
3   The second clips into the anchor and remains the second for the whole of the climb.
4   The original leader leads all the pitches.

In the first method – 'leading through' – the climbers alternate. 'Leading on' is often used where one member of the party is more proficient at climbing than the other, and so leads all the pitches. The setting up of intermediate stances may differ slightly, depending upon which method of ascent is chosen.

INTERMEDIATE STANCES
This term is used to describe a stance that is neither at the bottom or top of the cliff, but at some point up its height. For most bolted routes intermediate stances will be well positioned and at logical points, usually just under a rope length apart. They may make the most of natural features,

such as ledges, making things more comfortable for anyone who has to spend time there. Sometimes they consist of a couple of bolts on a smooth wall with little foot purchase, in which case a 'hanging stance' (see later in this chapter) will have to be deployed.

Stances with ledges
Most guidebook descriptions of route style and stance provision are very good, for example '6 pitches, all stances equipped', and so you will have a lot of information to hand prior to climbing. You may not, however, be able to find out if the stances are double bolts linked with a chain or two separate bolts, so take a sling with you so that you can equalise them if necessary. For the sake of the following descriptions it is assumed that the stance is situated above a reasonable ledge, and is made from two bolts linked with a chain to a central ring.

Tying in
Once you have arrived at the stance, make yourself safe. Your method will depend on certain circumstances – whether leading through or leading on and so on – but will normally come down to personal choice.

9

The multi-pitch crag of Saint-Jeannet, Maritime Alps

- **Method 1** Use your cow's-tail to clip yourself in (the simplest way). This can either be connected to the central ring, to a link in the chain nearby, or to one of the bolts. As you have no intention of loading it – and provided the bolts are not old and rusted – you can decide whether or not you will be safe enough clipping into just one side of the system and so do not need to clip into the equalised point.

- **Method 2** Tie in using the rope. A screwgate karabiner would be clipped into a suitable point on the anchor, and you clip into this, most likely with a clove hitch as the anchor is within reach. If the bolts are not linked with a chain, and you wish to achieve maximum security when tying in with the rope, a screwgate on each bolt and tying in with two clove hitches and a figure of eight on the bight back to your harness would do the trick.

Whilst getting yourself sorted out at the anchor it would be a good idea to clip an extender into the system so that you are protected by your belayer. This can be removed as soon as you have connected yourself to the system. It is very easy to feel secure on a ledge when you are actually some way above your last bolt and, with other things on your mind, mistakes can be made.

BELAYING THE SECOND
Once you are clipped into the anchor the next thing to consider is what method you wish to use to bring your second up: either direct (where the anchor system takes the load) or semi-direct (where you do). As we are on a stance with a good anchor and enough room to manoeuvre, a direct belay would probably be the preferred option. The advantage is that the belay device or mechanism can be clipped directly into the anchor, leaving you free to hold the rope, unencumbered by being tied tight to the rock.

USING A DIRECT BELAY
There are three choices of direct belay methods:

- Italian hitch
- Passive self-locking belay device
- Active self-locking belay device.

The Italian hitch works well in this situation, although it could tend to twist the rope over a length of a few pitches. One of its main advantages is that it can be tied off easily, allowing a belayer to bring up the second, tie her off and then lead onto the next pitch with only having to unclip the minimum amount of karabiners. Since the rope is used as the attachment device this keeps the whole system dynamic. This is important when belaying a leader, and has a distinct advantage over simply clipping in with a cow's-tail sling, which has no dynamic properties.

Using an Italian hitch

Clip a large HMS karabiner into the ring of the chain, with the gate facing out and the opening at the bottom. Clip the hitch into this karabiner, making sure that both live and dead ropes are not twisted. Maximum friction with the hitch is at the point where both ropes are parallel, thus to operate it effectively you must be in front of it. If the hitch is too far in front of you, it will be very difficult to get the correct braking angle. Pay the live rope into the hitch whilst taking out with the dead rope side, ensuring that one of your hands is on the dead rope at all times. The main criteria is to pay in with one hand and pull out with the other smoothly.

In the event of your partner slipping, holding on tight to the dead rope will prevent any being paid out. The hitch will most likely flip round the end of the karabiner and reform itself on the other side. This is perfectly normal and, as the knot is symmetrical, all part of the design. If your partner needs lowering down for any distance, put both hands onto the dead rope and feed it gently through, keeping the whole process smooth and controlled. You will have learned from being lowered from single-pitch routes that feeding a small amount of rope through a belay device feels like miles of slack on the other end, so keep it easy! Once your partner has regained a suitable position he can start climbing again. Feed the live rope into the hitch, whilst pulling out on the dead side, and the hitch will flip back through and reform on the taking-in side again.

MULTI-PITCH ROUTES

Note

It is important that an HMS karabiner is used here, as a D-shape screwgate could cause the rope to catch at the point of flipping through, totally jamming the system.

To tie off the Italian hitch – which can also be done with ease when it is loaded – use the following process. Using a bight of rope from the dead side, approx 60cm long, pass that round the live rope and through the resulting gap.

TYING OFF AN ITALIAN HITCH

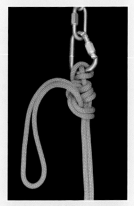

STEP 1 Make a slippery hitch.

STEP 2 Pull it tight to the karabiner, then tie two half hitches below it.

STEP 3 Finish off by pulling all the hitches up tight to the karabiner, leaving a long tail.

Pull this knot – a 'slippery hitch' – up tight to the karabiner. Now tie two half hitches with the loop around both sections of rope coming from the slippery hitch, also pulling them up tight to the karabiner. Make sure that the resulting loop of rope is around 30cm, to avoid any chance of it undoing.

Using a passive self-locking belay device

Many will choose to this system. These devices can be used to belay as normal – for example in a semi-direct belay situation when safeguarding a leader – but can be re-orientated to give a self-locking ability when clipped into an anchor and used as part of a direct system.

The biggest drawback of most of these devices is that it is extremely difficult to pay out rope if they are loaded. For instance, if used on a steep route, over a roof or bulge, and the second falls off and needs lowering some distance, it will take a while to construct a mechanism to facilitate this (see Chapter 4). Having said that, for situations where useful contact with the rock can always be made, such as slabs and easier grade climbs, paying out the rope is less of a problem and such a device is really useful. It also allows two ropes to be used, so if two people were following you up a route both could be clipped in – but probably not climbing – together. Because it admits two ropes, it also doubles up admirably as an abseil device.

Having arrived at the stance and made yourself safe, clip a screwgate karabiner to the ring on the chain. Onto this goes the appropriate part of the belay device, with any additional karabiners clipped in behind as per the manufacturer's instructions, incorporating the rope too.

To operate the device effectively it is a good idea to be a little in front of it, which makes pulling the rope through easier. You may have to sit down, which would also give your legs a rest. Feed the live rope into the device and take in on the dead rope, ensuring that you always have a hand on the latter. In the event of a fall the device will lock off automatically, most often by self-tightening the rope around the karabiner at the back.

Note

It is essential that this is not treated as a hands-off device; if you don't have hold of the dead rope at the time of loading it could start to slip through.

Using a passive self-locking belay device on a direct belay

Once your partner has regained his footing you can continue to belay as normal or, should he need slack rope, you can pay some out by adjustment of the karabiner at the back of the device – just how easy or tricky this is depends on the design.

Using an active self-locking belay device

This has the advantage that it is easy to pay rope out to a fallen second, in order for him to get down to a suitable point for starting to climb again. The device can be fixed to the ring on the chain, but it is essential that the lever mechanism is not anywhere near the rock. If the system is loaded and the rope moves the device to near the rock, there is a chance that the camming action – whereby the rope is squeezed by a moving part – could be compromised. This would not allow the rope to be held, with obvious consequences.

Note

Once again, although these mechanical belay devices lock off when loaded, this is not a hands-off method of belaying either a second or a leader. You may see others doing this, but don't be tempted.

Using an active self-locking belay device on a direct belay. It is essential that the cam is able to move freely.

USING A SEMI-DIRECT BELAY

You may decide that it is appropriate to use a semi-direct belay in order to safeguard the second. Its main disadvantage is that you are part of the system, and so affected by loading

Belay device and rope correctly orientated for belaying a second

should your partner take a slip. If you felt it were appropriate to belay in this manner, it would be a good idea to have the belay system dynamic throughout, right up to the anchor. Tying in with a rope is therefore preferable to clipping in with a cow's-tail. Although a semi-direct belay while clipped in with a sling would be acceptable when belaying a second, if he were to lead through a sling would provide a weak link in the safety chain. The rope, being tied into the anchor, would be far better. This could be set up by simply clipping a karabiner into the chain and attaching a clove hitch to this.

Sitting down is a good way to belay, as it will keep the anchor above hip height. Remember the ABC of climbing (anchor–belayer–climber), and that everything must be tight and in line. Make yourself snug on the anchor by taking in any slack at the clove hitch, but be in a position where you can communicate with, and preferably see, your partner. Also make sure that you are in line with the direction of pull; if off to one side you could be pulled over (particularly if standing up).

Once you are in position, clip the screwgate holding the belay device to the rope tie-in loop at your harness. This is better than having it on the abseil loop, as it keeps the whole system dynamic and makes more technical procedures, such as escaping the system, easier to carry out. Make sure that the rope comes up into the bottom of the device and exits from the top, thus keeping the rope correctly orientated. The different ways of belaying all involve feeding the live rope into the device and pulling out the dead one, all the time keeping one hand on the dead rope in case of a slip.

BELAYING THE LEADER FROM AN INTERMEDIATE STANCE

As the climber is getting ready to lead up from the stance, you will probably need to alter the set-up of the belay system. This will only take a few moments if you have planned ahead, and will greatly increase the safety of the leader.

It is usually very difficult and unwise to belay a leader from a direct belay. There are a number of reasons for this, the most important being:

- In the event of a fall the anchor chain/system will be pulled upwards

- Any device clipped to the anchor chain/system will thus be inverted and may become impossible to use
- It would be better to have as much shock absorption as possible in the system when belaying a leader, and a chain into a rock, or worse still an equalised sling, will provide none.

Therefore change a direct belay – ideal for protecting a second – into a semi-direct belay, which is far more appropriate for belaying a leader.

CHANGING FROM A DIRECT TO A SEMI-DIRECT BELAY SYSTEM

There is no difference whether the system used was passive, active or an Italian hitch: the basics remain the same. The only variation would be if the team were going to lead through or lead on.

Leading through (climbers alternate)

1 The second arrives at the stance and makes herself safe, most likely by clipping in with her cow's-tail.
2 The direct belay system can be dismantled.
3 The previous leader – now the belayer – gets himself organised. If he has thought ahead, he will have tied himself into the anchor with the rope, in order to provide a fully dynamic system. If he has not already done this he can do so now.
4 As long as the rope was neatly placed on the ground as the previous pitch was climbed, it will be in the right orientation for the next one. If not, a few seconds running the rope through, so that the leader's end comes out of the top of the pile and is on the correct side of the belayer, by his braking arm, will pay dividends later.
5 The belayer puts a belay device on his rope tie-in loop at his harness. As he is belaying a leader, it clips into the top of his loop. He could use either a standard belay device or an active self-locking type.
6 Having communicated, the new leader unclips her cow's-tail and continues up the next pitch.

Tip

Whether leading through or leading on, make sure that when you are at the ledge together you take all the extenders and other gear that you need for the next pitch from your belayer!

Belay device orientation when belaying a leader

Leading on

1   The second arrives at the stance and makes herself safe. This could initially be done by using her cow's-tail, but will end up with her tied onto it using the rope to a screwgate on the chain. If she was being belayed with an Italian hitch, this could be locked off and will be her anchor.

2   The leader, who is also to lead the next pitch, takes the second off the belay device. If he was connected to the anchor with the rope, he can remove this having first clipped himself in with his cow's-tail.

3   The second gets herself in a suitable position for belaying. She prepares a belay device by clipping it to the upper part of her rope tie-in loop at her harness, but does not clip the leader in yet.

4   As the rope is piled incorrectly, it needs 'turning round'. This is done by running it through, starting at the anchor end, into a neat pile at an appropriate point on the ledge and somewhere suitably close to the belayer.

5   Once the rope has been turned round, the belayer can clip the leader into her device.

6   Having communicated, the leader carries on up the route.

LEADING WHEN USING A SEMI-DIRECT SYSTEM

Although it might seem that everything is set up properly for belaying a leader when using this system (the belay device is already clipped to the belayer's harness), there are a couple of things that need doing. In particular, the orientation of the device needs changing, and the rope needs turning over as above. The other differences come about when choosing between leading through and leading on.

Leading through

1 The second arrives at the stance and makes herself safe, probably by clipping in with her cow's-tail. However, it is possible for the belayer to help here. He could tie a large overhand knot on the bight on the dead rope just next to the belay device, and this loop can then be clipped into the anchor.
2 The belayer, who will now become the second, takes the belay device off his tie-in loop and prepares it for the next pitch. This will involve turning it around so that the live rope comes out of the top, and clipping it back into his harness at the top of his tie-in loop.
3 The team now turns the rope around, running it through from the anchor side so that the rope to the leader comes from the top of the pile.
4 The belayer puts the leader's rope into his belay device.
5 Having communicated, the leader unclips her cow's-tail, or the overhand knot by the device, and leads on up.

Leading on

1 The second arrives at the stance and makes herself safe. This could initially be done by using her cow's-tail, but will end up with her tied onto it using the rope to a screwgate on the chain.
2 The leader, who is also to lead the next pitch, takes the second off the belay device. If he were connected to the anchor with the rope, he can remove this having first clipped himself in with his cow's-tail.
3 The second gets herself in a suitable position for belaying. She prepares a belay device by clipping it to the upper part of her rope tie-in loop at her harness, but does not clip the leader in yet.
4 As the rope is piled incorrectly, it needs turning round, starting at the anchor end, into a neat pile at an appropriate point on the ledge and somewhere suitably close to the belayer.
5 Once the rope has been turned round, the belayer can clip the leader into her device.
6 Having communicated, the leader carries on up the route.

STANCES WITH TWO SEPARATE ANCHOR BOLTS

There are a few extras to consider if the stance is equipped with two bolts and no connecting chain or cable. The main factor will be time, as you will need to link the bolts together using a sling in order to equalise them. Unless you are certain both bolts are absolutely secure, don't be

Tip

When at intermediate stances use the time to have a drink and maybe top up the sun cream or – if needed – put on a fleece. Do this before you start any of the changeover procedures, as it is best to not interrupt the sequence in case part is forgotten.

tempted to have your cow's-tail or rope connected to one and a direct belay device hanging on the other. In the event of a fall all the strain will be on one part of the system, which could fail. When you arrive at the stance protect yourself straight away with your cow's-tail, or clip in an extender and stay on belay while you work. Rig a sling appropriately and bring it down to a single point. You can now use this point for your own security and as a point from which to run the direct belay.

THE SECOND LEAVING THE STANCE

In preparation for leaving the stance you may be tempted to undo everything whilst waiting for the leader to get himself sorted above. This is not a very good idea, as you would only be on belay at the very last moment prior to climbing.

While the leader is setting up above, make sure that the rope will run freely when he comes to take it in. Get everything ready and make sure that all your gear is clipped to your harness and everything is stowed away in the rucksack (if one is being carried). Communication is vital, and in most instances the time to take the anchor apart – which will probably just involve unclipping a clove hitch and retrieving the karabiner – is after all the climbing calls when you have heard 'OK'. At this point the leader is ready to hold a fall, and should you slip prior to this he may not be prepared and you would be chancing injury. This is especially important on narrow ledges or if it is damp, when rock boots will have little or no traction. If you are not using the conventionally accepted climbing calls, always make clear to your partner at what point you will be expecting to be safeguarded from above.

HANGING STANCES

These are normally only found on the steepest and hardest routes, and even then there will usually be a small foot ledge on which you can get the weight off your harness to some extent. This will mean, however, that most of your weight will be committed to the anchor system and harness, so it is important to make sure that all is in order before setting out. Hanging in a harness for any length of time is very uncomfortable, especially with lightweight designs, manufactured to save every gram (often at the expense of padding). If you know that you will spend a lot of time 'hanging around', it may be worth taking a slightly heavier harness with good padding. Alternatively a lightweight belay seat can be used. It allows you to sit rather than hang, and shares the load better than a harness waist belt and leg loops. It is important to never use a belay seat without a harness, as it is purely an accessory for comfort and not a load-bearing part of the system.

Hanging stances are usually well equipped as the climbers who originally set up the route will have taken into account the fact that most of the belayer's weight will be suspended from it. Once you arrive at the stance, clip in straight away with the cow's-tail, a 60cm sling or rope being best for most situations. You can then use this as your sole connection to the anchor (most climbers will probably want to also clip the climbing rope in as well, using a screwgate karabiner and a clove hitch).

The rope management on hanging belays can be difficult to arrange, and takes some forethought. It may be tempting to let the rope hang down the crag in one massive loop, but this is not recommended. As mentioned above, there is a chance that the apex of the loop could become caught on a spike or tree, perhaps blown by the wind. Should this happen, the effect on your leader's morale will be remarkable! There are two other options available: flaking the rope in a manner so that it doesn't hang free, or using a rope keeper.

Flaking the rope

This method is the simplest to organise, but does mean that the rope is over the anchor attachment, where it could be in the way. The rope is flaked backwards and forwards over the rope between the belayer and the anchor, and allowed to hang down as far as might be appropriate. This allows the belayer to have complete control of how much rope is hanging down at his side, and he can pull as much as is required through to his belaying side.

Flaking the rope over the anchor rope to keep it tidy

Using a rope keeper

The second option is to use a rope keeper, designed to hold the rope in a flaked manner but out of the way of the anchor system. Commercially made rope keepers can be bought, usually consisting of a large split ring complete with a loop of tape for hanging on a harness or suitable part of the anchor. The rope is flaked through this, and will pull out as required without knotting. You could also use a sling to the same effect. Flake the rope across the anchor or somewhere appropriate – perhaps a knee – and then clip it into a 60cm sling, the ends of this being clipped into a suitable point,

Using a rope keeper to stop the rope hanging down the crag

Tip

When flaking the rope (either across the anchor ropes or through a keeper) start with larger loops and make them progressively smaller. This will ensure that the loops do not catch in each other and tangle.

such as one of the anchor bolts. This allows the rope to be pulled through as above.

DESCENT

Although some routes require you to walk off, sometimes for considerable distances, ladders and abseiling are the other options. If you know that you will have to walk off take a pair of lightweight shoes with you as rock boots are not only uncomfortable but have little traction on anything but rock.

Ladders

At some venues ladders may be positioned at suitable points along the crag. These are a useful method of descent, and a very good alternative to abseiling, especially in areas where the cliffs are busy. They may consist of one single length descending the whole height of the crag, a number of staggered sections, again going all the way, or one or two shorter sections positioned to allow easy descent of steep pieces of ground with the rest a scramble down.

Steel round-rung ladders are most commonly seen, but there are also via-ferrata-style steel step-hoops drilled into the rock to protect awkward sections. Although there is no reason why you should not just treat them like ladders at home (with respect, and after assessing their safety), some will choose to use a rope, if only to safeguard more nervous members of the party. If you need to do this set up a belay of some description, possibly an Italian hitch, on one of the upper ladder supports. Make sure that you are not getting in the way of other people waiting to descend unaided; allow them through if they turn up while you are getting the rope ready.

Abseiling

Descent will often be carried out by abseil. The technical side is covered in Chapter 10, but there are a number of factors worth emphasising here:

- Take your time and think through every stage of the descent.
- Plan ahead and note exactly where you are going, as the line down may not be obvious, or may not be the line you came up.
- In some areas abseil descents are deliberately set up away from the main climbing area to avoid the possibility of abseilers landing on climbers.

- When deploying the rope, call out before you throw it to warn other crag users. If you have noticed someone climbing below, make sure that they are in a safe position and are aware of what you are doing before throwing it off.
- Bear in mind the effect of the wind, as the rope will not drop in a straight line if there is a crosswind. You will have to drop the rope to one side of your intended line.
- When pulling the rope down onto an intermediate stance, remember that a length of rope the same height as the pitch you have just descended will drop down, possibly onto climbers some way below you.
- Check, check and then check again.

OTHER CONSIDERATIONS

When setting out on a multi-pitch route, take a moment to think how long it will take, what aspect it faces and how the descent needs to be organised. These will all affect your final decision as to what extra kit is needed. Planning ahead at this stage will make a big difference to both your comfort and the outcome of your climb. Any extra kit that isn't appropriate for clipping onto your harness or that will fit in a pocket could be carried in a small rucksack on the back of whoever is seconding at the time.

For routes of two or three pitches you probably don't need to worry too much about additional gear. However, if the route is four or more pitches, which could take a couple of hours or more to complete, think about the following.

Water

You will get through a lot of water during a day's climbing, especially if you are somewhere hot that catches the sun. Two hours into a 4-hour route under the full glare of the midday sun is not the place to start wishing you had some liquid with you.

Descent ladder at a multi-pitch crag

Keeping rehydrated is extremely important for the correct functioning of your body and, in particular, keeping your muscles operating. Little and often is the advice given. 'Tanking up' prior to leaving the ground, though favoured by some, does little to keep thirst at bay higher up the cliff. One additional problem is that if you over-hydrate early on your body will most likely wish to get rid of excess water at some stage during the climb – inconvenient for you and not particularly nice for your partner! Take a water bottle with you; some styles can be conveniently carried on the back of your harness. For a longer trip over a day, a couple of litres carried in a rucksack will be more appropriate.

Food

You would usually only take anything resembling a packed lunch on the longest routes, as the bulk and weight is too much to carry. However, a snack bar or two, tucked into a pocket, are well worth taking. They not only help stave off hunger pangs but can also provide much-needed energy when you start to flag. Chocolate and similar, although supplying you with a quick energy boost, does not fare well when the weather is hot. A better choice is a muesli or flapjack bar, which will not melt and will provide you with a good source of slow-release energy, making you feel full for longer.

A small rucksack should be sufficient for carrying extra food, water and the like on a multi-pitch route

Sunscreen

If the route is in the sun some form of sunscreen or sun block is important. This can be applied before you start climbing, and reapplication will be needed if you are climbing for several hours. Once you have applied it, find a patch of sandy or gravelly ground and give your hands a good scrub in order to remove any cream. Sunscreen is a very good lubricant, and not what you want on your fingers.

Sun hat

Think about taking a hat if the route is in the sun for some time. It is important that a sun hat is not used to the exclusion of a helmet, as it will not give you proper protection in the event of a slip or rock fall. A helmet will often be the choice of climbers heading for multi-pitch routes, as the terrain could be loose or present other hazards. However, if you choose not to wear one some type of protection against the sun is sensible, and a sun hat weighs very little and packs away small.

Sunglasses

These are essential when climbing in the sun, especially on rock such as limestone which reflect a lot of light. Make sure that they efficiently filter out UVA and UVB rays, but are not so dark that they mask hidden holds – a problem when there is great contrast between light and shadow. It is worth fitting them with a neck loop, enabling you to ditch them quickly yet safely should the route step out of the sun, perhaps when negotiating a deep chimney.

Descent shoes

You may have to walk off from the top of the route, which could take a couple of hours or more. Having a pair of shoes, other than rock boots, makes a lot of sense. Walking any distance in rock boots is never particularly pleasant, and if the ground is muddy or grassy they have no traction. You may elect to carry your own shoes with you, possibly in the rucksack or clipped to the back of your harness. There are lighter options available, such as some styles of kayaking and canyoning shoes, which also have the advantage of folding flat.

Head torch

Perhaps not on everyone's kit list for sport routes, but an item that can turn a great day into a great epic. If you know that the descent is quite long, and in particular if it involves going through forest, a torch will make life a lot easier if the climb has taken longer than you thought.

Spare clothing

For routes that have a marked change in elevation, or where the sun will be off and the ambient air temperature is cool, having a spare fleece as well as a hat and maybe gloves will go a long way to making you comfortable. Being stuck on a small ledge for what seems like hours, belaying someone involved on a hard pitch where the sun has gone in and the wind has picked up, can be a disheartening experience, and an extra layer will make all the difference.

Guidebook

If the pitch is particularly long or meandering, or the descent involves something more than an abseil directly down the route of ascent, it would be worth taking the guidebook. If you know which route you are heading to beforehand carry a photocopy of the appropriate page/s rather than the whole book if you are tackling a route that will take most of the day.

Abseiling from a multi-pitch crag in the French Alps

10 ABSEILING

On some routes abseiling, or rapelling, becomes necessary. This may be to facilitate descent in a multi-pitch situation, to retrieve equipment, or to follow another climber who has been lowered off. Whatever the reason you need to think about the most appropriate method in your particular situation.

DEPLOYING THE ROPE

In most cases there should be little problem in deploying the rope, letting it run out through the hands in a controlled manner. Care should be taken that it does not catch on anything; if this happens the problem can be sorted out during the abseil before passing the point at which the rope is snagged.

In some situations the rope needs to be deployed a little more forcefully. This may be because the wind will prevent it from being lowered gently, or maybe the line of descent is off vertical, taking a line slightly to one side. An efficient method in this situation is to deploy the rope overhand.

- From the anchor end, leave a couple of metres of slack and flake the rope backwards and forwards across the hand. Coiling it into loops should be avoided, as this will end up with the rope knotted.
- Once the rope has been fully flaked it should be divided into two parts, one in each hand.
- The hand holding the flakes leading to the end of the rope grips it around the middle, and it is then thrown over-arm towards its destination. You may need to adjust your aim to allow for the wind.
- The flakes in the other hand are held loosely and will be pulled off in turn, with the result that the rope will be deployed straight and without any knots.

An alternative, and one that works particularly well on long slabs, is to use the rope 'bomb' method.

- The rope is wrapped around the hand a few times, starting at the end away from the anchor.

Note

Whenever there is a possibility of other people climbing or walking in the area below your abseil point it would be courteous to shout 'Rope below' and pause for a moment before deploying. If an abseil is required at a busy crag, careful choice of the descent route will help avoid annoying, or even injuring, other users.

Tip

In a multi-pitch situation – and if the end of the rope is not touching a large ledge or the ground – it would be a good idea to knot the end to prevent climbers abseiling off it. The most efficient method is to tie an overhand knot in each of the two ends independently, about 1m up. This allows each section of rope to untwist while the climber descends, chasing out any kinks.

- Taking it off the hand, some more wraps are made around the initial coils.
- The wrapping is continued, changing the angle every few times, so that the finished article resembles a large ball of wool.
- Once enough rope has been wrapped, it is deployed down the route by rolling. It will undo itself without knotting and, on a slab, is capable of being aimed very accurately.

ABSEIL PROTECTION

Although abseils can be made by simply using the belay device (or indeed an Italian hitch) to provide friction and control the descent, the consequences of losing control are dire. A back-up system is often a good idea, particularly where the abseils are long or over awkward ground. The use of a prusik loop tied into a French prusik will be invaluable, and provides very good security.

The simplest option is outlined below.

- Having connected the abseil device to the rope, a French prusik is tied around the dead rope and connected to the leg loop on the relevant side: a right-handed climber will probably control the rope with his right hand during the abseil.
- During descent, the coils of the prusik can be held loose, but will slide up and lock off when released.

One concern here, however, is that if there is any chance that the prusik will be able to touch the top of the belay device, it will not grip. This could occur if the climber leans across in the opposite direction to the clipped leg loop to retrieve equipment, for instance, in which case the French prusik would not hold. A slight modification will prevent this.

- The abseil device is clipped to the harness and extended by 15–20cm. This can be done by using an extender with screwgate karabiners replacing the normal snapgates, or by using snapgates back-to-back to prevent accidental opening. Alternatively thread a sling through the harness, tied to the correct length.
- The dead rope has a French prusik tied around it, which is then clipped to the abseil loop, attached with a different karabiner to that holding the abseil device. It is important that the prusik loop is of suitable a length so that it cannot touch the top of the abseil device, otherwise it could fail and the system be rendered useless.

Tip
It is extremely useful to locate the centre of the rope, and this will often have been marked by the manufacturer with tape or coloured ink. However, if you need to mark the centre yourself, buy a specially formulated rope-marking ink. This is easily applied and will not affect the rope's performance. If choosing to use coloured tape take care that the adhesive used on the tape will not react with the rope. Avoid the use of fibre marker pens.

10

ABSEILING

Protecting an abseil using a prusik loop connected to a leg loop

Protecting an abseil using a prusik loop connected to the abseil loop

A cow's-tail rigged for an abseil

- Abseiling takes place with the rope between the abseiler's legs. One hand holds the prusik loosened, the other controls the descent by gripping the dead rope. When the French prusik is released, it travels a short distance up the rope and locks off, preventing any more rope from sliding through.

As this system is centrally clipped there is no chance of the prusik touching the top of the abseil device, even if the climber rotates sideways.

USING A COW'S-TAIL

To connect the abseil device to the harness, and at the same time provide a cow's-tail with which to clip into anchors during the descent, a 120cm sling can be used. This is very useful when descending multi-pitch routes.

- The sling is lark's-footed around the abseil loop.
- An overhand knot is tied 20–30cm away from the harness.
- The abseil device is clipped into this short loop.
- A French prusik is arranged as normal, clipped from the dead rope into the abseil loop.
- A screwgate karabiner is clipped into the end of the remaining larger loop. This can then be clipped onto a gear rack, ready for use.
- Once an intermediate stance has been reached, the screwgate at the end of the sling is clipped in. The abseil device and prusik can then be removed from the rope. The climber is therefore protected at all stages of the descent.

Tip

If it is found that controlling the descent is awkward and jerky, this can usually be solved by the addition of a karabiner clipped through the rope between the bottom of the abseil device and the connecting karabiner. This keeps the belay device a little above the karabiner, allowing the rope to run more smoothly.

Note

The French prusik is the best knot for protecting an abseil, although care should be taken to ensure that the prusik and the abseil device are correctly orientated. With the back-up prusik below the abseil device, the device takes the load of the abseiler when hanging, with the French prusik simply holding the dead rope in the brake position, which is correct. However, if the prusik is positioned above the abseil device this will have a very different effect of the loading of the system. With it above, the entire weight of the climber is suspended by the prusik, with the abseil device not being loaded at all. If this is a French prusik, there is a chance that should it be knocked it could fail and slip down the rope. If this happened, the prusik could melt through due to friction. If the climber decided to use a knot such as a klemheist instead (to stop the possibility of it slipping) it would be impossible to release once the weight of the climber was on it and might have to be cut in order to continue the descent.

ABSEILING WITH AN ITALIAN HITCH

An Italian hitch can be a useful tool in some circumstances, even though it tends to twist the rope during use. If a belay device is dropped from the top of a crag, for example, the Italian hitch may be the only other method for providing a controlled descent.

The rope rigged for an abseil using the Italian hitch

- The hitch must be used with an HMS karabiner. This should be clipped onto the abseil loop of the climber's harness so that the wide end is outermost and the back bar is on the side of the controlling hand. Thus, if the climber is right-handed, the gate of the karabiner will open to the left.
- As the rope will probably be doubled, one large Italian hitch is tied and the resulting four sections of rope clipped into the karabiner. If two separate hitches were tied, the system would jam after a short distance.
- It is important that the dead rope (held in the controlling hand) runs over the back bar of the karabiner (hence the note above about karabiner orientation). If it were to run across the gate there is a chance that it could unscrew the locking sleeve and unclip itself during the descent.
- Although maximum friction is achieved with the ropes parallel, so much friction is created with the two ropes that holding on tight to them in a normal, relaxed abseil position will give enough control for the descent.

JOINING ROPES

It may be that you are climbing using two ropes, utilising either the 'double' or 'twin' methods of leading and belaying. This would be more common on longer mountain routes where the pitches are sporadically bolted but the stances fully equipped, requiring the leader to place traditional gear as he climbs. There are a number of methods of joining ropes, but the two outlined below are the most common and will deal with the majority of situations. Joining ropes will normally allow you to double the length that can be abseiled in one go, compared with abseiling on a doubled-over single rope. Two 60m ropes enable a 60m abseil, whereas a single 60m rope only allows 30m to be descended.

Reef knot tied between a double fisherman's

Reef knot with double fisherman's
This is a solid knot, but does take a bit of practice to tie quickly. Its advantage is that it is very secure but will be relatively easy to untie after loading, as the fisherman's knots don't jam together due to the presence of the reef knot. The down side is that, should the rope be running over edges and around sections of rock, there is a chance that it will jam on retrieval as it is quite bulky. However, for most situations, where the rope will be running cleanly from the anchor, it is a good, safe choice.

Overhand knot
This knot has the advantage that it will present a smooth surface to the rock should it come across an obstruction whilst being retrieved. The knot, when tied, sits on one side of the rope and will tend to roll away from the rock when under tension. It is imperative that the knot is tidy, that it is pulled tight when tied, that the rope is running neatly through it, and that tail ends are no less than 50cm long.

If you want to make extra sure of the security of this system, you could tie a double overhand knot. The disadvantage is that you are starting to make a bulkier knot which has more chance of jamming. However, you may wish to accept this and end up with a knot that looks a bit bulky but still has some potential for pulling past obstructions. Once you have tied a single overhand knot as above, tie a second overhand knot butted tight up against it. Once again, keep it tidy, pull it tight and leave a good length of tail – 50cm is a good guideline.

(Above) Joining two ropes together using an overhand knot

(Below) Joining the ropes using two overhand knots butted together

RETRIEVING THE ROPE
Once down, you need to retrieve the rope. This will be much easier if you consider the options in advance, before descending, and sort out any problems from there.

In most situations there should be no trouble in pulling the rope through with reasonable ease. Care should be taken that there is no loose debris on ledges on the line that the rope will take, which could be dislodged. Out of courtesy, shout 'Rope' when starting to pull it down, making sure there is no one nearby who could be caught by the rope when it falls. If there was someone climbing a line close to yours, it would be polite to wait until they were well clear before starting the retrieval.

On most anchors, the rope will run smoothly. It is worth bearing in mind that if the ring through which the rope is running sits flat against the rock you need to pull on the correct side otherwise a lot of friction may be created. The rope should be pulled down on the side closest to the rock, which lifts the ring away from the surface slightly reducing friction. If the rope furthest away from the rock were pulled, this may have the effect of pressing the ring flat and causing it to stick. If abseiling on joined double ropes, make sure that the knot is placed on the side that is to be pulled. It may be a good idea to clip a loose running karabiner on the relevant rope to remind you which one to pull on once you are down.

The Italian hitch tends to twist the rope a little when abseiling for any distance, so a free-running karabiner will help. As you descend, the twists will keep the karabiner suspended some way above you. On the ground, as you start to untwist the rope, the karabiner can slide down, only reaching you when there are no twists left. You now know that the rope is unkinked and that the karabiner marks the side of the rope to be pulled.

AUTO-LOCKING BELAY DEVICE ABSEIL

An auto-locking belay device could be used in an abseil situation, but it should be remembered that these can generally only deal with one strand of rope. Often the choice will be made to remove the device and simply abseil with an Italian hitch or conventional passive device. However, it is still possible to abseil with one and then retrieve the rope. The simplest solution means that only a distance equal to just under half the rope's length can be descended, as the rope has to be doubled so that it can be pulled down. In other words, with a 60m rope the maximum distance abseiled is no more than 30m.

- The rope is threaded through the anchor to its middle point.
- A figure of eight on the bight is tied on the rope on one side of the anchor.
- A screwgate karabiner is clipped into this knot and then clipped around the rope on the other side of the anchor.
- The abseil device is clipped onto the rope that does not have a knot in it, taking care to check that the correct side is being used.

(Above) **Pulling the correct way on a flat-ring abseil rope retrieval**

(Below) **Karabiner suspended above an Italian hitch on an abseil**

10

ABSEILING

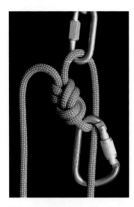

(Above) **Set-up for retrieval when abseiling with a device that can only be used on a single rope, such as the Grigri**

(Below) **Set-up for retrieving the rope using a thin pull line**

- Once the descent is complete and the abseil device removed, pulling on the other side of the rope, the one with the knot in it, allows it to be retrieved.

FULL-LENGTH ABSEIL

If this is going to be necessary the team will probably be aware of it before the ascent starts, and requires them to carry another length of rope. This needs to be as long as the main rope, although it can be considerably thinner and lighter as it will not be used to hold anyone's weight.

- Pass the end of the full-weight rope through the anchor and tie a figure of eight on the bight on the end.
- The thinner length has a figure of eight tied in it as well, and the loops in both ropes are clipped together with a screwgate karabiner.
- This screwgate is then clipped into the main rope below the anchor.
- The main rope is abseiled on. Once down, the thinner rope is pulled and the system can be retrieved.

Note

As the rope used to facilitate the full-length abseil may be quite thin, care must be taken to ensure that it does not tangle when being deployed. The wind can cause a problem here as the lighter rope or cord will tend to blow around and possibly jam off route. If this were a possibility it would be sensible to have the rope prepared in a manner by which it can pay itself out as the first person descends. Flake it into a stuff sack, which can then be clipped onto the climber's harness. Once the first person is at the end of the abseil, he can hold onto the rope or otherwise secure it in some fashion to ensure that it does not blow out of reach.

Tip

Whenever both climbers are at a stance and pulling the rope through, it must be ensured that there is no chance of dropping it down the crag and becoming stranded. Having the rope clipped to a suitable part of the anchor before starting to pull it down will prevent this.

Appendix 1
CLIMBING GRADES AND GUIDEBOOKS

Climbs the world over are graded according to their difficulty. The French grading system is used across much of Europe, with other countries and continents having their own preferred method. It can take a little time to get used to the differences, but after climbing a few routes you will soon get the idea as to how they compare to the local grades you are used to.

CLIMBING GRADES
The table below gives a comparison of climbing grades for a selection of countries round the world. These are for guidance only, as there is some leeway in interpretation, particularly on the harder routes. Resources such as the Internet will provide information on graded lists from countries not included here, and will clarify local anomalies and discrepancies. However, the equivalent gradings shown below are accepted by most climbers.

The table might look confusing, but includes a number of countries for the purposes of comparison. The bold numbers are the benchmark technical grading for British traditional climbing – for instance, you would expect to find VS 4c as standard, or E2 5c (although there will be a lot of leeway either side of these grades).

As for sport-climbing grades, only one figure is given – 4, 6a and so on. This is because of the different approach to climbing bolted routes compared to placing gear whilst on the lead. For instance, in the UK the grading system has two parts: the first being letters – VS, E1; the second numbers – 4c, 5c. The first part indicates the seriousness of a route, the second the hardest technical moves. Thus, a VS 4c would be the benchmark grade for that level of climbing, but a VS 5a would indicate harder technical climbing but with a seriousness factor more usually associated with an easier route, meaning it will be well protected.

Sport-climbing grades only have one figure because the climb will usually be equipped with bolts both at regular intervals along the pitch and at the anchors. This means that the seriousness factor (which appears as part of the UK system) is not indicated. Routes are graded for the overall difficulty of the climb, and so there may be anomalies between

FRENCH/SPORT	UK SERIOUSNESS	UK TECHNICAL	RUSSIA	NORWAY	USA	UIAA	SOUTH AFRICA	POLAND	AUSTRALIA
-	Moderate	–	III	1	5.1, 5.2	I, II			4, 5
2	Difficult	**3a**	III+	1, 2	5.3, 5.4	II		I	5, 6
2	Very Difficult	3a, **3b**	IV-	1, 2	5.4	II+		I	6, 7, 8
2+	Hard Very Difficult	3b, **3c**	IV	2, 3	5.4, 5.5	III-		II	8, 9
3	Mild Severe	3c, **4a**	IV, IV+	3	5.5, 5.6	III		II, III	9, 10, 11
3+	Severe	**4a**, 4b	IV+	3, 4-	5.6	III+, IV-	13	IV	11, 12
3+, 4	Hard Severe	4a, **4b**, 4c	IV+	4	5.7	IV-	14	V-	12, 13
4	Mild Very Severe	**4b**, 4c	V-	4	5.7	IV, IV+	14, 15	V-, V	13, 14
4, 4+	Very Severe	4b, **4c**, 5a	V-	4+	5.7, 5.8	IV+	15, 16	V	14, 15
5, 5+	Hard Very Severe	**5a**, 5b	V	5-	5.9	V-, V, V+	17, 18	V+	15, 16, 17
5+, 6a	E1	5a, **5b**, 5c	V	5, 5+	5.10a, 5.10b	VI, VI	19	VI	17, 18, 19
6a+, 6b	E2	5b, **5c**, 6a	V+	6-, 6	5.10c. 5.10d	VI+, VII-	20, 21	VI+	19, 20, 21
6b, 6b+	E3	5c, **6a**, 6b	V+	6+, 7-	5.10d, 11a	VII-, VII	22, 23	VI.1+	21, 22
6c, 6c+, 7a	E4	**6b**, 6c	VI-	7	5.11b, 5.11c, 5.11d	VII+, VIII-	24, 25	VI.2	22, 23
7a, 7a+, 7b	E5	6b, **6c**	VI	7+	5.11d, 5.12a, 5.12b	VIII, VIII+	26, 27	VI.3	23, 24, 25
7b+, 7c, 7c+	E6	6c, 7a	VI+	8-, 8	5.12c, 5.12d, 5.13a	IX-, IX	27, 28	VI.3+, VI.4	25, 26, 27
8a, 8a+	E7	6c, 7a, 7b	VI+	8+, 9-	5.13b, 5.13c	IX-, X	29, 30, 31	VI.5, VI.5+	27, 28, 29, 30
8b, 8b+	E8	6c, 7a, 7b, 7c	VII	9	5.13d, 5.14a	X, X+	32, 33	VI.6, VI.6+	29, 30, 31
8c, 8c+	E9	7a, 7b, 7c, 8a		9+	5.14a, 5.14b	XI, XI	33, 34	VI.7	31, 32
9a	E10	7b, 7c, 8a			5.14c, 5.14d	XI+, XII			32, 33

two adjoining routes of the same grade. For instance, two routes may both be graded 6b+, with one having a couple of hard moves part way up but the other having easier moves sustained for its entire length.

Grades will always be subjective. At 2m tall I would find a 6b route totally different in character and difficulty to someone considerably shorter; sometimes I'll win, sometimes I'll lose. Also the grading on crags – even those geographically close and covered by the same guidebook – can feel remarkably different when you are actually climbing them: a 6a route on one may feel like a grade 5 on another. Although it will take you a while to work out which level you are happy with, and to what grade you aspire, a little perseverance will pay dividends. You will soon learn what target grade to head for when setting out for a day's climbing.

GUIDEBOOKS

You will probably want to obtain a guidebook covering the area you are visiting. There is a lot of information available these days – in particular on the Internet – about where to climb, what the crags are like, access, history and so on. A few pages of information can be downloaded from the Internet, particularly if new routes have recently been completed. However, a guidebook will often be your first port of call, as it will provide all the relevant information plus certain extras.

Book-style guides are often lavish productions with information not only about the climbing but also how to get there, places to stay and even where to enjoy an after-cragging drink. The most useful guidebooks will include a number of 'topos', topographical drawings or photographs of the crags with the routes marked on by dotted or coloured lines. These will also indicate the position of intermediate stances and lower-off points, as well as abseil stations, ladders and walk-off information. Parking and directions on how to get there are important. The better books will also have a wealth of peripheral information about the crag, often shown in icon form at the head of the page.

UNDERSTANDING 'TOPOS'

The topo of 'la roche à Roche' (see below), a crag in the south of France just outside Monaco, is typical of a well-written and very informative guide. The main picture is a topo of the crag with the routes marked and numbered, the top circles being the location of the lower-offs. Pasted onto the topo is a graph showing how many routes at what grade are available: three at grade 4 and seven at grade 5. The

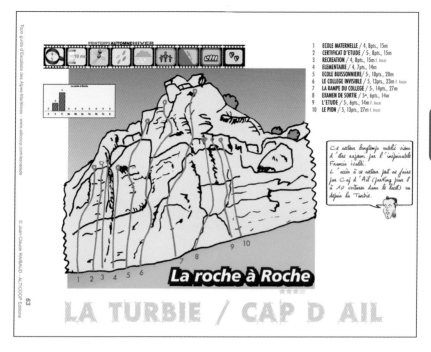

1   ECOLE MATERNELLE / 4, 8pts., 15m
2   CERTIFICAT D'ETUDE / 5, 8pts., 15m
3   RECREATION / 4, 8pts., 15m F. bwzo
4   ELEMENTAIRE / 4, 7pts., 14m
5   ECOLE BUISSONNIERE/ 5-, 10pts., 20m
6   LE COLLEGE INVISIBLE / 5, 13pts., 23m F. bwzo
7   LA RAMPE DU COLLEGE / 5, 14pts., 27m
8   EXAMEN DE SORTIE / 5+, 6pts., 14m
9   L'ETUDE / 5, 6pts., 14m F. bwzo
10 LE PION / 5, 13pts., 27m F. bwzo

Topo of La roche à Roche

route names are at the top right-hand side, as well as the grade, how many bolts are available and the length of the route from bottom to top in metres (remember: for lowering off your rope needs to be over twice this length!). Just below a cartoon character gives a little more relevant crag information.

Along the top of the page is a useful row of icons, giving information specific to the crag. These indicate, running from left to right, that:

- It faces south.
- The walk-in takes 10 minutes.
- That it is best climbed in spring, autumn and winter (along with the south-facing icon, indicating that it would be too hot in summer).
- It is suitable for a family.
- The climbing is predominantly on steep slabs.
- Finger strength will be useful.
- Finally, that the routes are mainly equipped with closely placed expansion bolt hangers (as opposed to resin anchors).

The topo of Le Fantome of Saint-Jeannet, also in the south of France (see below), shows information relevant to multi-pitch routes. This may look a little more confusing, but

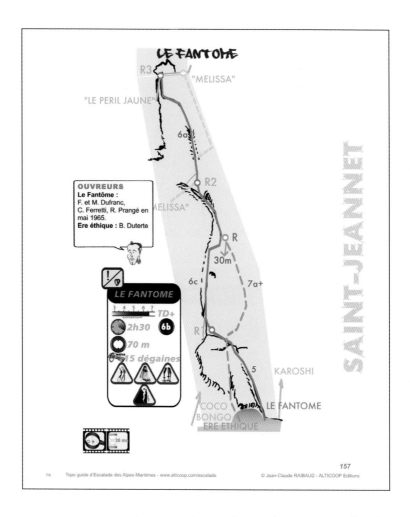

Topo of le Fantome

when comparing it to the actual crag on site it all makes sense. The line of the topo shows the route in relation to others nearby, how many pitches, the placement of belay stances and any variations. Major rock features, such as cracks and ramps, are also shown. Each pitch has a grade, and these are put together to give an overall grade. The icons at the bottom tell us that it is west facing and will be reached in about 30 minutes. The box captioned 'Le Fantome' provides some very important information. The top-left corner icon shows that the route has little gear in place and can be classed as 'adventurous', meaning that gear has to placed on the lead in a traditional manner. The grade is shown below the box title, along with the time that a competent party should take to complete the 70m-long climb. Fifteen extenders are recommended, along with some other gear in the triangular icons: slings, wires and camming devices. The scary-looking final icon at the bottom of the box indicates that the cliff is loose in places, implying that a helmet would be a sensible precaution.

Tip

In some areas thieves deliberately target climbers' cars, safe in the knowledge that they are busy elsewhere. If you are somewhere this has been a problem – the guidebook will often advise you if this is so – don't leave anything in the vehicle. Leave the glove box open and unfix the rear luggage cover so that there is obviously nothing worth taking. Planning ahead for the day will avoid having to leave excess gear in the car, possibly tempting the unscrupulous.

FINDING YOUR WAY AROUND

So, you have your guidebook and have decided which crag to head for – what next? It's worth relating any driving and parking directions given in the book to a road map in order to iron out any initial problems, as guidebook sketch maps can be remarkably inaccurate and should be used for guidance only. Once parked, there will probably be a description of how to get to the crag. This may be glaringly obvious – the cliff may be only a couple of metres away – or may involve a walk of an hour or more.

Guidebooks come in all shapes and sizes, and are an invaluable source of reference

You arrive at the crag. What now? Unless there is one small cliff at the location, climbing areas are often divided into 'sectors'. These could be as simple as 'east' and 'west', or have more cryptic names such as 'sector heroic'. Follow the directions to your required sector. As you approach it, take a minute to step back and relate the topo in the guide-book to the actual crag. Look for obvious features such as corners, roofs, cliff-top trees, lines of bolts and other clues that will indicate where you are in relation to the routes you wish to climb. Look for lines of bolts and relate these to the topo. Finally, many cliffs have the names of the route either painted on the rock or written on small plaques set into it. These will be at chest or head height, and will contain the route name and usually the grade.

It is worth selecting a gearing-up point that is flat, not too far from the base of the route and, if it is sunny, in the shade in order to keep food cool. On multi-pitch routes – where you will be away from your gear for an hour or two – remember to take important items such as wallet and car keys with you, leaving only the minimum kit behind.

SELECTED SPORT-CLIMBING VENUES

The ultimate in roadside cragging

Appendix 2
SELECTED SPORT-CLIMBING VENUES

The following venues have been chosen to demonstrate the wide variety of climbing that is available across the world. Although most are in Europe, sport climbing is now a global activity, and hopefully these descriptions will encourage you to investigate the many thousands of bolted crags available worldwide.

Country:	England
Crag/region:	Portland, Dorset
Guidebook:	*Dorset* Mark Glaister and Pete Oxley (Rockfax, 2005)
Description:	The Isle of Portland is home to a collection of crags rather than just one, but all are within a short distance of each other. They have been extensively bolted, and the area gives a huge selection of routes from very easy right through to 'as hard as you like'. The rock is limestone, which offers a variety of climbing styles depending upon which area is visited, and due to its sheltered nature climbing is possible here year-round.

Country:	Australia
Crag/region:	Blue Mountains, New South Wales
Guidebook:	*Rock Climbs in the Upper Blue Mountains* (SRC, 2000); *Blue Mountains Selected Climbing Areas* Martin Percher and Simon Carter (publisher unknown, 2000)
Description:	The Blue Mountains are an eroded sandstone plateau 100km west of Sydney, and can be reached by a drive of about 1.5hrs. A number of crags make up the area, offering single and multi-pitch climbs from grade 13–33. Climbing is possible year-round, although the summer months can be unbearably hot at some venues. Plenty of water, sunscreen and sunhat are essentials.

Climbing at the slab area, Portland. This route is only graded 3 but is one of the most photogenic in the country.

The La Loubière sector at Turbie. Clean limestone and plenty of bolts make this a superb year-round venue.

Country: France

Crag/region: Turbie, Cote de Azur.

Guidebook: *L'escalade dans les Alpes-Maritimes* Jean Claud Raibaud (Alticoop, 2004)

Description: Turbie offers a fine selection of routes, mainly single pitch, on a selection of limestone crags overlooking the Mediterranean Sea. Situated just outside Monaco, the area offers classic south-of-France scenery and weather, with plenty of space so that you can feel alone even on holiday weekends. Most of the routes are generously bolted and lower-offs are, for the most part, *in situ*, and usually consist of a double bolt to chain with welded ring or clip-in connector. There are about 15 crags, all very accessible and giving a tremendous day's sport.

Country: Spain

Crag/region: Peñas del Rey, Costa Blanca

Guidebook: *Costa Blanca* Alan James and Mark Glaister (Rockfax, 2005)

Description: The Peñas del Rey is a series of striking towers, home to a number of excellent routes in the grade 5–6 range. There are a variety of short and long routes, almost all being superb quality. The region also hosts many other crags worth a visit, making the Costa Blanca region one of the most important and popular sport-climbing venues in Europe.

Country:	Scotland
Crag/region:	Benny Beg, Perthshire
Guidebook:	*Scottish Sport Climbs* Joanna George et al (SMC, 2007)
Description:	This is a very short and compact crag, with nearly all the routes below 6a, making it ideal for beginners or those wanting to keep their grade at an amenable level. It is well bolted and has a very short 1min walk in! Although all the routes could be climbed in a single day, it offers a good introduction to sport climbing. Facing south, it is also climbable throughout most of the year.

Country:	Mallorca
Crag/region:	Sa Gubia, in the west of the island
Guidebook:	*Mallorca* Alan James and Mark Glaister (Rockfax, 2005)
Description:	Sa Gubia offers a variety of climbs on a large range of crags facing a variety of aspects. Generally well bolted, the cliffs offer both single and multi-pitch routes. The classic route is up the magnificent prow of Sector Espolon, a seven-pitch 4+, 240m in length. Although this is bolted in part, a rack of gear will be needed for some sections.

Country:	France
Crag/region:	Les Gaillands, Chamonix valley
Guidebook:	*Crag Climbs in Chamonix* François Burnier and Dominique Potard (Vamos, 2005)
Description:	The collection of crags that make up Les Gaillands is a short walk from the centre of Chamonix, an important centre for European Alpinism. The crags offer single and multi-pitch routes across the spectrum of grades, with over half being below 5+ level. Generally well bolted, there are still sections where the protection is well spaced – beware! The crag can be busy at times although it is possible to escape the crowds by heading for one of the more remote areas, only a few minutes' walk away. Facing southeast, it can be very hot in summer, although there are tree-shaded areas for respite.

The Great Prow of Sa Gubia, home to some excellent multi-pitch routes at amenable grades

Country:	Switzerland
Crag/region:	Anzeindaz, east of Lac Leman
Guidebook:	*Escalades Vaud, Chablais, Bas, Valais* Claude and Yves Remy (Sanetsch, 2004)
Description:	This area is located in a lovely mountain setting and comprises a number of crags around the Col des Essets. The col is home to a number of boulders, some of which have been bolted. Crags nearby, such as La Corde, offer a number of easy routes from 2c upwards. However, beware as the limestone is particularly sharp here – an older thick rope would be better than a very thin new one. The walk to the col takes around 1hr, with the crags dotted around a little further on.

Country:	Italy
Crag/region:	Corno Piccolo, Apennines
Guidebook:	*Gran Sasso* Fabrizio Antonioli and Fabio Lattavo
Description:	The Corno Piccolo offers a huge range of routes across the grades, with many available in the 4 and 5 region. However, these are long routes and some may not be well bolted between stances, so it would be sensible to carry a light rack of a set of wires and a few cams. The guidebook gives estimated times for a fit and competent party, and routes can easily take 6 or 7hrs or more. Take plenty of food and water, along with a head torch each early or late in the season.

Bouldering at Col des Essets, in a beautiful location by the bolted crags and boulders of Anzeindaz

Les Fees Meres, 6b,
Saint-Jeannet

Country:	USA
Crag/region:	Penitente Canyon, Colorado
Guidebook:	*Rock Climbing in the San Luis Valley* Bob D'Antonio (Falcon, 1999)
Description:	The Penitente Canyon area is home to a host of accessible sport routes, all well bolted and on stunning rock formations. The range of grades, from 5.2–5.13c, means that there is something for everyone, and there are a number of other sport-climbing venues nearby. There is great scope for further development if you are keen, and a mass of excellent bouldering available if you have energy to spare!

Country:	France
Crag/region:	Saint-Jeannet, Alpes Maritimes
Guidebook:	*L'escalade dans les Alpes-Maritimes* Jean Claud Raibaud (Alticoop, 2004)
Description:	I make no apology for including another French crag, as some of the most spectacular climbing can be found here. The Saint-Jeannet region covers a huge area and offers single and multi-pitch climbs across the grades. Ally this with a variety of superb settings, particularly on the longer routes, and you have a venue with something for everyone.

Interesting rock formation on 'How the West was won', 5.9, Penitente Canyon

Climbing on the spectacular Il Fiamma, Val Bregaglia

Country:	Italy
Crag/region:	Spazzacaldeira, Albigna
Guidebook:	*Bernina and Bregaglia Selected Climbs* (Alpine Club)
Description:	The Spazzacaldeira is in the heart of a huge area of climbing venues, and commands superb views over the Val Bregaglia. Nearly all the routes are multi-pitch, with the carrying of a light rack being necessary on most. There are many other peaks and venues in the region, making it a good base for a prolonged stay.

3
APPENDIX

GLOSSARY

Certificat D'Etude, Turbie

Appendix 3
GLOSSARY

Abseiling (rappelling, rapping) To descend the rope, usually after the completion of a climb, often using a system of protection for safety.

Active self-locking belay device A belay device with moving parts, such as a Grigri or SUM. These devices will rely on a loading on the rope to operate properly and, although will usually hold a fall 'automatically', are not designed to be used as 'hands off' devices. Great care should be exercised in using them, as it takes a while to learn the method of operation, particularly when lowering and abseiling.

Aid To use some equipment to help make a move up the rock. A climb may contain one or more points of aid. In its simplest form it will entail clipping a sling or similar into a bolt and pulling on it or using it as a foothold. Routes with more than one point of aid may require a sequence of moves using bolts or traditionally placed kit. Many routes that once required aid have now been climbed without it, in other words 'free'. This often affects the grade of the route, making the overall difficulty much harder.

Alternate leads (leading through, swinging leads) Used in a multi-pitch situation, where one person will climb a pitch, belay, and bring up the second person, who will then become the leader for the next pitch, and so on.

Artificial route Often used to describe a route that has been 'squeezed in' between two others. The guidebook description may say something like 'don't use the rib on the left', which would otherwise be a totally natural thing to do. As you will be climbing with certain areas out of bounds, the whole route would feel artificial.

Back bar This is the long bar opposite the gate of a karabiner, and where most of the strength is aligned. D-shape karabiners are designed to hold the rope, sling or other items clipped in a position aligned as close as possible to the back bar, giving maximum strength.

Back-clipping This is where a leader clips a karabiner, most often on an extender, in the incorrect manner. It is important that the rope from the belayer comes up to the back of the karabiner and out through the front. This is so that when the leader moves on and up, the karabiner and extender keep the correct orientation. If it is back-clipped – the rope goes into the front and up and out from the back – there is a chance that the rope could unclip in the event of a fall, or the extender become undone from the bolt.

Bail out To come down from a climb before it is completed. This may be because it is too hard, the weather has changed, darkness is falling, or a myriad of other reasons. Bailing out will usually involve abseiling or rapping off, but can also be used to describe a single-pitch climb where the team has had enough and lowers off.

Batmanning A leader pulling up on the rope coming past him to the belayer, following a fall, in order to regain his highpoint. Could also be used when bottom-roping for the same reason. The name comes from the 'Batman' programmes of the 1970s, where the plucky duo were seen climbing buildings hand over hand, albeit blatantly on a flat set with the camera tilted through 90°. Similar to 'yarding'.

Beer towel A useful piece of kit, ideal for wiping the soles of rock boots prior to climbing. Although beer towels are traditional climbers' gear, any small piece of rough towelling will do.

Belay station The place where the rope is controlled from and the belayer is positioned. Often used to describe intermediate stances on multi-pitch routes.

Beta Knowledge of a route. To have 'beta' is to have been told or found out – perhaps from previous climbers, abseil inspection and so on – about key holds, resting positions, places from which to clip gear and the like. Usually only of relevance for those climbing at the hardest grades, in the eyes of purists having beta will detract from the quality of the ascent.

Beta flash To climb a route cleanly from bottom to top with no falls but with some prior knowledge. This may include knowing about key holds or gear placements. One of the purest styles of ascent, it is overshadowed only by an on-sight flash.

Bolt-on An artificial hold that has been bolted or glued onto the cliff. This will usually be done because that part of the route is featureless, and having a bolt-on helps maintain the grade at a constant level. At the other extreme entire outdoor crags which would otherwise be featureless can be bolted in order to provide somewhere for people to climb. Bolt-ons are either commercially made, usually of a resin compound, or natural rock drilled, bolted and glued into position.

Bottom-roping A method of belaying where control of the rope – the belayer – is positioned at the bottom of the climb. The rope will run up from the belayer, through a karabiner system at the top of the route, then back down to the climber. This allows routes harder than the climber's normal grade to be attempted, and is often used when introducing novices to climbing. It is most frequently seen after a leader has completed a route, lowered off stripping the extenders out as he goes, and the rope left in place for the second and any subsequent climbers to use.

Chain A frequently used system of linking bolts at a lower-off at the top of a route. This allows two bolts to be connected in such a way that the lowest point of the chain, often equipped with a metal ring or a maillon, can be used by climbers in a manner that means any loading on the system is shared equally by each of the anchors. Chain has the advantage over cable or other methods in that it is easy to rig, cheap, long-lasting and provides plenty of scope for clipping into through the links. It is also very adjustable and can be easily equalised and cut to size during its installation.

Choss Collective term for leaf mould, twigs, mud, grass, loose rocks and the like. If a line is said to be 'chossy' it means that it is not clean rock and might be quite dirty in sections, or over the entire route.

Crater To hit the ground after a fall. 'Cratering' is a lighthearted way of describing a very serious situation. The term came from the hole left by cartoon characters when they fall from a height.

Crux The hardest part of a route. Most will have a crux move that will feel a little harder than those coming before or after it, although some climbs might have a 'second crux' at a later stage.

D-shape karabiner These have a pronounced curve at each end, at the side adjoining the back bar. This concentrates any load in this area, the strongest part of the construction.

Dead rope The rope that is held in the hand of the belayer, and which comes out from the belay device. It is by holding the dead rope in the correct manner that falls can be stopped and lowers carried out. It is also the controlling side of the device used when abseiling. The golden rule of climbing is that the dead rope is never dropped, even for an instant. Self-locking belay devices, although mostly working by themselves, are not 'hands off' devices, and the dead rope should always be held.

Direct belay A belay where all the loading is transferred directly through to the anchor. Clipping a karabiner into a chain on an intermediate stance and using an Italian hitch from there, for instance, means that it is a direct belay. An active self-locking belay device clipped to a sling around a substantial tree root when bottom-roping would fall into the same category. The advantage is that any loading is directed to the anchor, and the belayer is free to move about (within reason). A disadvantage is that the solidity of the anchor needs to be beyond question; if there were any doubt subsequent loading could cause anchor failure.

Dogging The action of a leader falling onto protection as he works out a sequence of moves. The leader may fall a number of times as the hard section is practised, and then 'batman' or 'yard' his way back to his highpoint. To 'dog' a route is to climb it by using these methods, not seen as being a clean ascent but perhaps part of the practice section of working towards a redpoint.

Extenders Also known as quick-draws or tie-offs, these are lengths of sewn sling with a karabiner at each end, used to clip into protection. Extenders come in a variety of sizes and widths, but for the clipping of bolts will generally be kept quite short, around 10–15cm. It is worth having a couple of longer extenders to hand on the harness in case off-line bolts have to be used, or to extend those tucked under bulges or other projections. The snapgate karabiners on an extender will often be one straight and one bent gate, but this is down to personal choice.

Free climbing Climbing without resorting to aid tactics. Free climbing is often confused by non-climbers with soloing, which does not involve the use of any ropes or other safety devices at all.

Ground fall potential A hazardous situation, where a slip by the leader could result in him hitting the ground from some distance up. This is always a problem before the first bolt is clipped, and potentially whilst clipping the second. With the latter there could be enough slack in the system so that should the leader slip the rope is long enough to let him hit the ground. Sparsely spaced bolts could also lead to ground fall potential, even from quite high up after a couple have been clipped.

HMS karabiner (pear-shape karabiner) These have a wide curve to one end and are designed for use with the Italian hitch in particular. They should be used instead of D-shape karabiners for this purpose, as the lack of a tight bend at the end of the back bar allows the hitch to move freely forwards and back. Several ropes can be clipped in and they generally have a wide gate opening. They are not as strong as a D-shape, as the loading could be some distance from the back bar.

Hanger The part of a bolt through which a karabiner is clipped. This term is usually reserved for the bent metal plate fixed to the outside of an expansion bolt.

In situ Equipment that is already in place prior to the leader climbing the route. Bolts are almost always *in situ*, although in some circumstances a team may need to carry a couple of hangers to place on bolt heads if these have been removed through vandalism or by design. Pieces of rope tied around threads are also said to be *in situ*, but should be treated with caution as they may be old and affected by UV degradation and other factors.

Leading on Used in a multi-pitch situation where the same person will be leading the entire route. He leads the first pitch, belays up the second, leads the next pitch, and so on.

Leading through (alternate leads, swinging leads) Used in a multi-pitch situation, where one person will climb a pitch, belay, bring up the second person who will then become the leader for the next pitch, and so on.

Live rope The rope that comes out of the front of the belay device and goes to the climber. Control of the live rope is important to ensure that it does not snag in use, but control of the dead rope is the more crucial.

Lob To fall off for some distance, usually reserved for describing a leader fall.

Lower-off a) The equipment at the anchor end of a climb that allows the rope to be fixed through it and the climbers to descend while protected from above. A lower-off will typically consist of a chain linked to two bolts, with a ring or maillon for the rope or a karabiner to be connected to. A single bolt, or two independent ones, will do the same job.

b) A climber descending by committing his weight to the rope and it being paid out by the belayer. A climber could lower off from the top anchor, or be lowered off from an intermediate bolt, probably with an extender through it, to rest or change leads on a hard route.

Maillon A steel karabiner-like link with a screw device covering the opening, but often without the hinged gate. These are used extensively in the rigging of lower-offs as they are cheap and easy, and the gate can be almost permanently shut tight with the use of a spanner and left in place. A small maillon will often be carried at the back of the leader's harness as it could be used to connect the rope to a bolt should he need to come down off the climb part way through and does not wish to sacrifice a karabiner.

On sight The cleanest style of ascent, a climb completed with no falls or prior knowledge and at the first attempt. The only information is that seen from the base of the climb, and no other beta has been collected. An on-sight flash ascent is the purest style of climbing, aspired to by most and much revered at the highest levels.

Passive self-locking belay device A device used to safeguard a climber, most commonly the second, that works by being clipped into a direct anchor system and locks the rope automatically when loaded. As there are no moving parts, the locking mechanism is usually provided by clipping a karabiner through a loop of rope that will cause it to jam when pulled.

Passive belay device A belay device that typically consists of a tube or rounded box shape, normally with two slots, through which the rope can be run. The braking effect is created by the belayer holding onto the dead rope and controlling its slippage through the body of the device. Other than the rope passing through it, there will be no other moving parts.

Pear-shape karabiners Another name for HMS karabiners, with a wide curve to one end that allows efficient use of knots such as the Italian hitch.

Practice Rehearsing a move or sequence of moves prior to completing a route. This could be done on a bottom rope or on the lead, and may be done prior to attempting a redpoint ascent.

Quick-draw Another word for an extender.

Rap Short for **rappel**, and an alternative to abseil. To 'rap off' a route is to descend by rappelling or abseiling, either because the top has been gained or the team has decided to bail out.

Redpoint The ascent of a route after prior practice. The climber might decide to bottom-rope the climb or to lead it as far as he can, possibly falling a number of times in the process. Once he is happy that he can do all the moves without falling, the rope will be pulled down and he will lead it from the bottom up. Extenders may be placed when leading or, more commonly, left *in situ* and clipped on the way past.

Screamer A very long leader fall. The closeness of bolts usually prevents particularly impressive screamers from taking place, but they can occur if the bolts are sparse or if traditional gear has been placed and rips out.

Screwgates Karabiners with a locking sleeve that can be done up to prevent accidental opening. These should be used anywhere that failure of the system could be catastrophic, such as on main anchors, bottom-rope rigs and the like.

Semi-direct belay The belay process where the rope is controlled through a device connected to the belayer, such as in their tie-in loop or abseil loop. In the event of the belayer being secured to an anchor, the belayer can take some of the load even though most of the force is transmitted through to it.

Spotting Looking out for the safety of a climber when they are near the ground, often prior to clipping the first bolt. Spotting is most usually done by the second, who will be in a braced position with arms outstretched, ready to field the climber should he slip. The idea is not to catch the climber but to keep him on his feet and prevent him from falling backwards and tripping over a hazard.

Stance The place from which belaying takes place. A stance may be at the bottom of a route, at the top, or at various points along its length (intermediate stances). An intermediate stance will usually be equipped with bolts suitable for belaying from; a stance on the ground may have nothing at all.

Swinging leads (leading through, alternate leads) Used in a multi-pitch situation, where one person will climb a pitch, belay, bring up the second person who will then become the leader for the next pitch, and so on.

Top-roping A rope system where the belayer is controlling the rope when positioned at the top of a route or cliff. This is often used where a number of people want to try the climb, such as in a group activity. It is less common in sport climbing, as the tops of routes often do not extend to the top of the cliff. For this reason, bottom-roping is often the preferred option.

Traditional climbing Climbing a route placing all the protection equipment whilst on the lead. Wires, cams and slings will be placed by the leader at regular intervals, then stripped out by the second. Traditional gear is sometimes used on sport climbs, more often on longer, multi-pitch routes between stances that may be equipped with bolts. If this approach is needed, it will usually be made obvious by the guidebook description.

Wire gate The gate part of a karabiner that is not solid in section but formed by bent wire. As well as being lighter than a solid-section gate, it also means that there are no springs to help gate closure. The ends of the wire gate are drilled into the body of the karabiner in such a manner as to give a natural spring, negating the need for other moving parts. A particular advantage is that, as the gate has very little mass, there is little chance of it being opened by the vibration and whiplash effect of the rope during a fall.

Working a route To spend time on a climb, getting the sequence of moves right, often prior to making a redpoint ascent. Climbers attempting the hardest grades may work a route for some considerable time, perhaps over a number of months or more, before finally gaining a redpoint ascent.

Yarding A leader pulling up on the rope coming past him to the belayer, following a fall, in order to regain his highpoint; it could also include pulling up on extenders or other gear. Could also be used when bottom-roping for the same reason. Similar to batmanning.

Yo yo To make the ascent of a climb after falling and being lowered back to the ground one or more times, without unclipping any protection already placed. This style of ascent allows the climber to rest between attempts at climbing the route in its entirety, often used when making his way to redpointing it.

Z-clipping Clipping the rope from below the previous extender into the one above. This means that the rope from the belayer runs up to the top extender, down through it to the lower one and up to the climber's harness. Only possible if the bolts are close together, it creates an enormous amount of drag and also means that the leader is not safeguarded by the higher bolt. As such, it needs to be sorted out straight away, simply by unclipping the lower bolt so that the rope can run through and be held by the upper one.

Attempting a hard redpoint ascent

INDEX

The main reference is in **bold**

INDEX

NOTES

LISTING OF CICERONE GUIDES

BACKPACKING
The End to End Trail
Three Peaks, Ten Tors
Backpacker's Britain Vol 1 – Northern
  England
Backpacker's Britain Vol 2 – Wales
Backpacker's Britain Vol 3 –
  Northern Scotland
The Book of the Bivvy

**NORTHERN ENGLAND
LONG-DISTANCE TRAILS**
The Dales Way
The Reiver's Way
The Alternative Coast to Coast
A Northern Coast to Coast Walk
The Pennine Way
Hadrian's Wall Path
The Teesdale Way

FOR COLLECTORS OF SUMMITS
The Relative Hills of Britain
Mts England & Wales Vol 2 – England
Mts England & Wales Vol 1 – Wales

UK GENERAL
The National Trails

BRITISH CYCLE GUIDES
The Cumbria Cycle Way
Lands End to John O'Groats – Cycle
  Guide
Rural Rides No.1 – West Surrey
Rural Rides No.2 – East Surrey
South Lakeland Cycle Rides
Border Country Cycle Routes
Lancashire Cycle Way

CANOE GUIDES
Canoeist's Guide to the North-East

**LAKE DISTRICT AND
MORECAMBE BAY**
Coniston Copper Mines
Scrambles in the Lake District (North)
Scrambles in the Lake District (South)
Walks in Silverdale and
  Arnside AONB
Short Walks in Lakeland 1 – South
Short Walks in Lakeland 2 – North
Short Walks in Lakeland 3 – West
The Tarns of Lakeland Vol 1 – West
The Tarns of Lakeland Vol 2 – East
The Cumbria Way &
  Allerdale Ramble
Lake District Winter Climbs
Roads and Tracks of the Lake District
The Lake District Angler's Guide
Rocky Rambler's Wild Walks
An Atlas of the English Lakes
Tour of the Lake District
The Cumbria Coastal Way

NORTH-WEST ENGLAND
Walker's Guide to the
  Lancaster Canal
Family Walks in the
  Forest Of Bowland
Walks in Ribble Country

Historic Walks in Cheshire
Walking in Lancashire
Walks in Lancashire Witch Country
The Ribble Way

THE ISLE OF MAN
Walking on the Isle of Man
The Isle of Man Coastal Path

**PENNINES AND
NORTH-EAST ENGLAND**
Walks in the Yorkshire Dales
Walks on the North York Moors,
  books 1 and 2
Walking in the South Pennines
Walking in the North Pennines
Walking in the Wolds
Waterfall Walks – Teesdale and High
  Pennines
Walking in County Durham
Yorkshire Dales Angler's Guide
Walks in Dales Country
Historic Walks in North Yorkshire
South Pennine Walks
Walking in Northumberland
Cleveland Way and Yorkshire Wolds
  Way
The North York Moors

**DERBYSHIRE, PEAK DISTRICT,
EAST MIDLANDS**
High Peak Walks
White Peak Walks Northern Dales
White Peak Walks Southern Dales
Star Family Walks Peak District &
  South Yorkshire
Walking In Peakland
Historic Walks in Derbyshire

WALES AND WELSH BORDERS
Ascent of Snowdon
Welsh Winter Climbs
Hillwalking in Wales – Vol 1
Hillwalking in Wales – Vol 2
Scrambles in Snowdonia
Hillwalking in Snowdonia
The Ridges of Snowdonia
Hereford & the Wye Valley
Walking Offa's Dyke Path
Lleyn Peninsula Coastal Path
Anglesey Coast Walks
The Shropshire Way
Spirit Paths of Wales
Glyndwr's Way
The Pembrokeshire Coastal Path
Walking in Pembrokeshire
The Shropshire Hills – A Walker's
  Guide

MIDLANDS
The Cotswold Way
The Grand Union Canal Walk
Walking in Warwickshire
Walking in Worcestershire
Walking in Staffordshire
Heart of England Walks

SOUTHERN ENGLAND
Exmoor & the Quantocks
Walking in the Chilterns
Walking in Kent
Two Moors Way
Walking in Dorset
A Walker's Guide to the Isle of Wight
Walking in Somerset
The Thames Path
Channel Island Walks
Walking in Buckinghamshire
The Isles of Scilly
Walking in Hampshire
Walking in Bedfordshire
The Lea Valley Walk
Walking in Berkshire
The Definitive Guide to
  Walking in London
The Greater Ridgeway
Walking on Dartmoor
The South West Coast Path
Walking in Sussex
The North Downs Way
The South Downs Way

SCOTLAND
Scottish Glens 1 – Cairngorm Glens
Scottish Glens 2 – Atholl Glens
Scottish Glens 3 – Glens of Rannoch
Scottish Glens 4 – Glens of Trossach
Scottish Glens 5 – Glens of Argyll
Scottish Glens 6 – The Great Glen
Scottish Glens 7 – The Angus Glens
Scottish Glens 8 – Knoydart
  to Morvern
Scottish Glens 9 – The Glens
  of Ross-shire
The Island of Rhum
Torridon – A Walker's Guide
Walking the Galloway Hills
Border Pubs & Inns –
  A Walkers' Guide
Scrambles in Lochaber
Walking in the Hebrides
Central Highlands: 6 Long
  Distance Walks
Walking in the Isle of Arran
Walking in the Lowther Hills
North to the Cape
The Border Country –
  A Walker's Guide
Winter Climbs – Cairngorms
The Speyside Way
Winter Climbs – Ben Nevis &
  Glencoe
The Isle of Skye, A Walker's Guide
The West Highland Way
Scotland's Far North
Walking the Munros Vol 1 –
  Southern, Central
Walking the Munros Vol 2 –
  Northern & Cairngorms
Scotland's Far West
Walking in the Cairngorms

Walking in the Ochils, Campsie Fells and Lomond Hills
Scotland's Mountain Ridges
The Great Glen Way
The Pentland Hills: A Walker's Guide
The Southern Upland Way
Ben Nevis and Glen Coe

IRELAND
The Mountains of Ireland
Irish Coastal Walks
The Irish Coast to Coast

INTERNATIONAL CYCLE GUIDES
The Way of St James – Le Puy to Santiago cyclist's guide
The Danube Cycle Way
Cycle Tours in Spain
Cycling the River Loire – The Way of St Martin
Cycle Touring in France
Cycling in the French Alps

WALKING AND TREKKING IN THE ALPS
Tour of Monte Rosa
Walking in the Alps (all Alpine areas)
100 Hut Walks in the Alps
Chamonix to Zermatt
Tour of Mont Blanc
Alpine Ski Mountaineering Vol 1 Western Alps
Alpine Ski Mountaineering Vol 2 Eastern Alps
Snowshoeing: Techniques and Routes in the Western Alps
Alpine Points of View
Tour of the Matterhorn
Across the Eastern Alps: E5

FRANCE, BELGIUM AND LUXEMBOURG
RLS (Robert Louis Stevenson) Trail
Walks in Volcano Country
French Rock
Walking the French Gorges
Rock Climbs Belgium & Luxembourg
Tour of the Oisans: GR54
Walking in the Tarentaise and Beaufortain Alps
Walking in the Haute Savoie, Vol 1
Walking in the Haute Savoie, Vol 2
Tour of the Vanoise
GR20 Corsica – The High Level Route
The Ecrins National Park
Walking the French Alps: GR5
Walking in the Cevennes
Vanoise Ski Touring
Walking in Provence
Walking on Corsica
Mont Blanc Walks
Walking in the Cathar region of south west France
Walking in the Dordogne
Trekking in the Vosges and Jura
The Cathar Way

PYRENEES AND FRANCE / SPAIN
Rock Climbs in the Pyrenees
Walks & Climbs in the Pyrenees

The GR10 Trail: Through the French Pyrenees
The Way of St James – Le Puy to the Pyrenees
The Way of St James – Pyrenees-Santiago-Finisterre
Through the Spanish Pyrenees GR11
The Pyrenees – World's Mountain Range Guide
The Pyrenean Haute Route
The Mountains of Andorra

SPAIN AND PORTUGAL
Picos de Europa – Walks & Climbs
The Mountains of Central Spain
Walking in Mallorca
Costa Blanca Walks Vol 1
Costa Blanca Walks Vol 2
Walking in Madeira
Via de la Plata (Seville To Santiago)
Walking in the Cordillera Cantabrica
Walking in the Canary Islands 1 West
Walking in the Canary Islands 2 East
Walking in the Sierra Nevada
Walking in the Algarve
Trekking in Andalucia

SWITZERLAND
Walking in Ticino, Switzerland
Central Switzerland – A Walker's Guide
The Bernese Alps
Walking in the Valais
Alpine Pass Route
Walks in the Engadine, Switzerland
Tour of the Jungfrau Region

GERMANY AND AUSTRIA
Klettersteig Scrambles in Northern Limestone Alps
King Ludwig Way
Walking in the Salzkammergut
Walking in the Harz Mountains
Germany's Romantic Road
Mountain Walking in Austria
Walking the River Rhine Trail
Trekking in the Stubai Alps
Trekking in the Zillertal Alps
Walking in the Bavarian Alps

SCANDINAVIA
Walking In Norway
The Pilgrim Road to Nidaros (St Olav's Way)

EASTERN EUROPE
The High Tatras
The Mountains of Romania
Walking in Hungary
The Mountains of Montenegro

CROATIA AND SLOVENIA
Walks in the Julian Alps
Walking in Croatia

ITALY
Italian Rock
Walking in the Central Italian Alps
Central Apennines of Italy
Walking in Italy's Gran Paradiso
Long Distance Walks in Italy's Gran Paradiso
Walking in Sicily

Shorter Walks in the Dolomites
Treks in the Dolomites
Via Ferratas of the Italian Dolomites Vol 1
Via Ferratas of the Italian Dolomites Vol 2
Walking in the Dolomites
Walking in Tuscany
Trekking in the Apennines
Through the Italian Alps: the GTA

OTHER MEDITERRANEAN COUNTRIES
The Mountains of Greece
Climbs & Treks in the Ala Dag (Turkey)
The Mountains of Turkey
Treks & Climbs Wadi Rum, Jordan
Jordan – Walks, Treks, Caves etc.
Crete – The White Mountains
Walking in Western Crete
Walking in Malta

AFRICA
Climbing in the Moroccan Anti-Atlas
Trekking in the Atlas Mountains
Kilimanjaro

NORTH AMERICA
The Grand Canyon & American South West
Walking in British Columbia
The John Muir Trail

SOUTH AMERICA
Aconcagua

HIMALAYAS – NEPAL, INDIA
Langtang, Gosainkund & Helambu: A Trekkers' Guide
Garhwal & Kumaon – A Trekkers' Guide
Kangchenjunga – A Trekkers' Guide
Manaslu – A Trekkers' Guide
Everest – A Trekkers' Guide
Annapurna – A Trekker's Guide
Bhutan – A Trekker's Guide
The Mount Kailash Trek

TECHNIQUES AND EDUCATION
The Adventure Alternative
Rope Techniques
Snow & Ice Techniques
Mountain Weather
Beyond Adventure
The Hillwalker's Manual
Outdoor Photography
The Hillwalker's Guide to Mountaineering
Map and Compass
Sport Climbing: Technical skills for climbing bolted routes
Rock Climbing: Introduction to essential technical skills

MINI GUIDES
Avalanche!
Snow
Pocket First Aid and Wilderness Medicine
Navigation

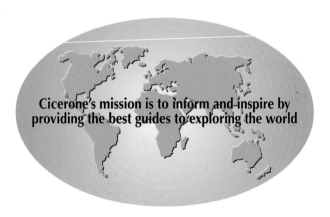

Cicerone's mission is to inform and inspire by
providing the best guides to exploring the world

Since its foundation over 30 years ago, Cicerone has specialised
in publishing guidebooks and has built a reputation for quality
and reliability. It now publishes nearly 300 guides to the major
destinations for outdoor enthusiasts, including Europe, UK and the
rest of the world.

Written by leading and committed specialists, Cicerone guides are
recognised as the most authoritative. They are full of information,
maps and illustrations so that the user can plan and complete a
successful and safe trip or expedition – be it a long face climb, a
walk over Lakeland fells, an alpine traverse, a Himalayan trek or a
ramble in the countryside.

With a thorough introduction to assist planning, clear diagrams,
maps and colour photographs to illustrate the terrain and route,
and accurate and detailed text, Cicerone guides are designed for
ease of use and access to the information.

If the facts on the ground change, or there is any aspect of a guide
that you think we can improve, we are always delighted to hear
from you.

Cicerone Press
2 Police Square Milnthorpe Cumbria LA7 7PY
Tel:01539 562 069   Fax:01539 563 417
e-mail:info@cicerone.co.uk   web:www.cicerone.co.uk